VANCOUVER PUBLIC LIBRARY

The borrower is responsible for returning this book in good condition. Please examine before taking out and report any damage.

*Literature and Gentility
in Scotland*

*

*To Hazel
who was in at the conception
and the delivery*

LITERATURE AND GENTILITY
IN SCOTLAND

THE ALEXANDER LECTURES
at the University of Toronto, 1980

*

DAVID DAICHES

AT THE UNIVERSITY PRESS, EDINBURGH

*   *

*

© David Daiches 1982
Edinburgh University Press
22 George Square, Edinburgh

Set in Monotype Poliphilus
by Speedspools, Edinburgh
and printed in Great Britain by
Clark Constable Ltd

British Library Cataloguing in Publication Data

Daiches, David
   Literature and gentility in Scotland
   1. Scotland — Civilization
   I. Title
   941.1   DA772

ISBN 0-85224-438-X

Contents

*

PREFACE

The following chapters represent the Alexander Lectures delivered at the University of Toronto in March 1980. They are printed here exactly as they were delivered: I have made no attempt to change the speaking voice into written exposition, believing that there is something to be said for retaining the original sense of communication to a living audience. I have added a few footnotes, identifying quotations from modern critics, but I have kept these at a minimum.

David Daiches
Edinburgh

*

I

THE END OF COURTLINESS

The transition from an aristocratic ideal of courtliness to a bourgeois ideal of gentility is well documented in European culture. It can be seen in English literature very clearly in the period between Sir Thomas Hoby's translation of Castiglione's *Il Cortegiano* in 1561 and the essays of Addison and Steele in the *Tatler* and *Spectator* between 1709 and 1712. It is fascinating to trace the modification of the Renaissance ideal of the courtier—its gradual transmutation under the influence of middle class ambitions and new ideals of prudence and middle class morality—in the host of works that appeared in sixteenth- and seventeenth-century England, with such titles as *Youth's Instruction, Civil Conversation, The English Gentleman* (and *The English Gentlewoman*), *The School of Vertue,* and to see how it emerges in, say, the fiction of Samuel Richardson in the following century and in the novels of Jane Austen at the beginning of the nineteenth century. This development is a commonplace of cultural, social and literary history. Something parallel happened in Scotland, but there were special factors present in Scotland which were not present in England or indeed elsewhere in Europe. These make the Scottish situation unusually interesting.

The most important of these factors was the sudden departure of the Court in 1603, when James VI of Scotland inherited the throne of England and went south to become also King James I of England, thus removing Scotland's chief if not only source of patronage of the arts—the royal Court. He took court poets and musicians with him, and some of these flourished in England, the poets learning to use English instead of Scots and writing for an English audience. It is true that James returned to Scotland, but only once, in spite of his promise on leaving to come back every three years. His sole return visit took place in 1617. He entered Edinburgh on 16 May of that year amid traditional ceremony that had not been seen in Scotland since his entry into the city in 1579 at the age of thirteen. The 1617 celebrations included the recital of a fulsome Latin eulogy, and a poem in English by William Drummond of Hawthornden entitled "The Muses' Welcome to the High and Mighty Prince James, . . . at his Majesty's happie Returne to his old and native Kingdome of Scotland". Drummond also published another poem to mark this occasion, entitled 'Forth Feasting: a Panegyricke to the Kings Most Excellent Majesty', in which he presented the River Forth as rejoicing 'That my much-loving Prince is come againe'. He addresses James directly in terms of high flattery:

O *Vertues* Patterne, Glorie of our Times,
Sent of past Dayes to expiate the Crimes,
Great King, but better farre than thou art greate,
Whome State not honours, but who honours State,
By Wonder borne, by Wonder first enstall'd,
By Wonder after to new Kingdomes call'd,
Young kept by Wonder neare home-bred alarmes,
Old sav'd by Wonder from pale Traitours Harmes,
To bee for this Thy Raigne which Wonders brings,
A King of Wonder, Wonder unto Kings.
If *Pict, Dane, Norman,* Thy smooth Yoke had seene,
Pict, Dane, and *Norman,* had thy Subjects beene:
If *Brutus* knew the Blisse Thy Rule doth give,
Even *Brutus* joye would under Thee to live:
For Thou Thy People dost so dearly love,
That they a Father, more than Prince, Thee prove.

Drummond, who lived from 1585 to 1649, was only
eighteen when James left Scotland and did not embark
seriously on his career as a poet until some ten years later. Not
being an established poet by 1603 he had not to face the
decision whether to accompany James to England or to
remain in Scotland. Though his home remained in Scotland,
he travelled abroad, visiting London and spending two years
in France. He soaked up all the English, French, Italian and
Spanish poetry and drama he could lay his hands on and,
while living quietly for most of his life on his country estate
near Edinburgh with his books and music, wrote poetry in
English under a variety of English and European influences.
He did not write in Scots apart from some early 'prentice
poetry written in imitation of James's 'Castalian band' of
poets who, though now dispersed, were still remembered. But
as he grew to maturity, nourished by Renaissance ideals of
courtliness and craftsmanship he absorbed through his reading, he found nothing remaining in Scotland that could provide any inducement to embody these ideals in poetry written
in the Scots language. So he wrote in English, with his eye
more on English than on Scottish poets, rather a solitary
figure, an oddity even, a Scottish poet without a natural
linguistic base in his own country. That situation was to
become less uncommon, but Drummond in his day was in
many ways a man apart.

Drummond welcomed James back to Scotland in English
courtly verse. Just over half a century earlier, in 1561,
Alexander Scott had welcomed Queen Mary to Edinburgh
on her return from her long stay in France with a courtly poem
in Scots:

> Welcum! illustrat ladye, and oure quene;
> Welcum! oure lyone with the floure de lyce;
> Welcum! oure thrissill with the lorane grene;
> Welcum! oure rubent roiss vpoun the ryce;
> Welcum! our jem and joyfull genetryce;

Welcum! our beill of albion to beir;
Welcum! oure pleasand princes, maist of pryce;
God gif the grace aganis this guid new-yeir.

This combines, in a manner that is not uncommon in older
Scottish poetry—in Dunbar for example—admiration and
admonition. The poem is signed in the final stanza 'thy
sempill servand Sanderris Scott', concluding on a note of
loyalty and service. If we accept Helena Shire's conjecture
that Alexander Scott the poet was identical with the con-
temporary musician of the same name—and we know of
course that poetry, music and dance were closely associated
at the Scottish Court, especially in the Franco-Scottish cultural atmosphere that first flourished when James V brought
home his French wife Princess Madeleine, and, again, when
after her early death he married Marie de Lorraine—then he
would have had a close association with the Chapel Royal
and with the atmosphere of royal service and royal patronage
associated with it. In any case, we know that Scott's poems
were often found with music. Mrs Shire describes him as 'the
courtly makar whose words were sung, and whose songs were
dances'. He was well established as poet by 1568, when
George Bannatyne compiled his manuscript collection which
is the major source for the text of his poems. He saw three
reigns, active at the Court of James V, rendering poetic and
perhaps also musical service to Queen Mary, and surviving
to see the Court of James VI. In his old age he was a respected
representative of an older style which had links with the
mediaeval courtly love tradition. But he was also a con-
spicuously *Scottish* poet. When, in his poem of welcome to
Queen Mary, he signed himself 'Sanderris Scott', he was
emphasising his Scottishness, for 'Saunders' was then, as it
was for Sir Walter Scott, the generic term used for a Scotsman,
as Pat later became used for an Irishman, Taffy for a Welsh-
man and Jock (which eventually succeeded Saunders) for a
Scotsman. In the long career of Sanderris Scott we can trace

4

the development of one of the last phases of the courtly tradition of Scottish poetry in its association with music and dance.
At least, we could trace it if all the sources still existed, which
unfortunately they do not.

How far Scott's courtly poem of welcome to Queen Mary
was in an older Scottish courtly tradition is not easy to say,
for little of courtly song and music in Scotland has survived
from earlier periods. The wedding of Princess Margaret of
Scotland to King Eric II of Norway in 1290 was celebrated
in a Latin song; the earliest celebratory songs in Scots that
exist are those that formed part of the celebrations of 'the
marriage of the thistle and the rose', i.e. the marriage of James
IV of Scotland to the Princess Margaret Tudor, daughter of
Henry VII, in 1503. Even these survive only in fragments, but
we do know that they were part-songs. 'Now fayre, fayrest of
every fayre . . . Welcum of Scotland to be Quene'. Dunbar
certainly celebrated the marriage in his elaborate poem in the
dream-allegory tradition, 'The Thrissil and the Rois'. But
this is a far cry from a celebratory part-song. More akin to
Scott's welcome to Queen Mary is Dunbar's 'New Year's
Gift to the King' with its mixture of compliment and advice.
It opens

My Prince, in God gif the guid grace,
Joy, glaidness, comfort, and solace,
Play, pleasance, myrth, and mirrie cheir,
In hansill of this guid new year.

where the recurring last line of each stanza is echoed in
Scott's recurring last line, 'God gif the grace aganis this guid
new-year'. Dunbar's poems addressed to James IV, however,
are certainly not songs, and though he was in a sense a court
poet and considered himself a servant of the King—and an
ill-requited one at that—his attitude to his royal master was
ambivalent to say the least.

But whatever the significance of royal patronage at the Court
of James IV, it is certainly true that at the Court of James V

and at certain periods in the reigns of his successors there was a lively tradition of court poetry, associated in its earlier phases with court song and dance, and that this tradition could not survive the removal of the Court in 1603. Even in the century between the 'marriage of the thistle and the rose' and the Union of the Crowns the tradition flourished only intermittently, because of the troubled political and religious situation. The years immediately after the disastrous battle of Flodden in 1513, leaving an infant king on the throne, were not conducive to an active court culture, but, when the king (James v) grew older, there is clear evidence of his involvement in poetry and music. The poet David Lindsay was tutor to the young prince and a participant in the amusements of the Court. An entry in the treasurer's accounts for 12 October 1511 shows the expenditure of £3 4s for blue and yellow taffeties 'to be a play coat to David Lyndsay for the play playit in the king and queen's presence in the Abbey of Holyrood' and there are also entries of quarterly payments of an annual salary of £50 for duties at Court. His account of his relation to the young King is given in his 'Epistil to the Kingis Grace' prefixed to his poem 'The Dreme', while in 'The Complaynt' he recalls

> How, as ane chapman beris his pak,
> I bure thy Grace upon my bak,
> And sumtymes, strydlingis on my nek,
> Dansand with mony bend and bek.
> The first sillabis that thow did mute
> Was PA, DA LYN. Upon the lute
> Then playit I twenty spryngis, . . .

The young King's activities seem to have included a considerable amount of what censorious historians have called debauchery as well as courtliness, and there are legends of his going around the country in disguise, sleeping with his female subjects. These activities do not seem to have decreased after his assumption of personal authority in 1528—perhaps they began then—and it is interesting that, as well as participating in a courtly culture where music, dance, masquerades and love songs both in the old courtly love tradition and in a time-less tradition of simple bawdry all flourished, he also associ-ated himself with the folk tradition both by his wanderings in disguise and by perhaps composing poems describing popular festivities: at least both 'Peblis to the Play' and 'Chrystis Kirk on the Grene' used to be attributed to him as well as the lively popular poems 'The Gaberlunzieman' and 'The Jolly Beggar'.

But it is the courtly not the popular James V that concerns us here. It was the Franco-Scottish style of his court culture after his first marriage in 1536 that re-established a tradition of courtly song, dance and music in mutual association. How far that tradition survived continuously after the King's death in 1542 following his humiliation at the defeat of a Scottish army by the English at Solway Moss is difficult to say. He left a newborn daughter, Mary Queen of Scots, and a country torn between conflicting claimants to the regency—one of whom was his widow, the French Marie de Guise—and bitter politico-religious disputes between an emerging Pro-testant faction oriented towards England and a Catholic faction oriented towards France. Some court-song and dance and a variety of courtly ceremonies seem to have marked the French Queen Mother's circle, and certainly after the young Queen Mary's return from France to Scotland in 1561 courtly song, dance and music must have been encouraged, though we know little about it in spite of our knowledge of her patronage of her music-loving secretary David Riccio. It was the courtly tradition of singing, dancing and music-making that so offended Protestant feeling, which was against the whole tradition of Courtly Love and its sophisticated accom-paniments in the arts as well as the popular tradition of seasonal festivities, May Day ceremonies, Robin Hood plays and ballad singing. In November 1587 the Town Council of Edinburgh issued one of its many proclamations expelling

burgh 'all menstrallis, pyperis, fidleris, common
, and specially of badrie and filthy sangs, and siclyke
ounds and maisterless persouns quha hes na seruice
nor honest industrie to leif by'. If the courtly tradition was
removed, already under attack from Protestants who associated it with a corrupt Roman Catholic culture, and at the
same time the popular tradition was under attack for its pagan
feeling and general impropriety, it was not going to be easy
to find a substitute for the artistic patronage of the Court when
it left Scotland for good in 1603.

Court song was part-song, and part-writing for voices or
instruments or both was traditionally known in Scotland as
musik fyne. We now know that *musik fyne* has a longer history
in Scotland than used to be thought. Thanks to the researches
of Helena Shire and Kenneth Elliott we have some precise
notions of 'what possible ways there were in sixteenth-
century Scotland of combining words and music with other
elements, dance, spectacle, contest, joust or ceremony, in order
to make a "devising" for courtly participation or entertainment of a simple or more complex nature—the danced song,
the sung romance, the interlude or *cartel*, the wedding psalm
or mourning "mynd".'[1] Although we have little specific evidence for words and music and dance going together in
sixteenth-century Scotland, evidence from France and England makes it clear that this was part of the courtly tradition,
with music, either vocal or instrumental, in four parts. Some
of the songs that were sung in this way have survived in
interesting mutated form in the collection commonly known
as *The Gude and Godlie Ballatis* which includes secular love
poems, both courtly and popular, re-cast in a Protestant
religious mould, so that a courtly love song beginning with
the traditional mirthful May morning and continuing with an
appeal to the poet's lady to be kind to him is transmuted into

Intill ane myrthfull Maii morning
Quhen Phebus did up spring

Walkand I lay in ane garding gay
Thinkand on Christ sa fre;
Quhil meiklie for mankynde
Tholit to be pynde
On Croce Cruellie, La La.

We could almost translate this into its secular original even if
we did not have a mid-seventeenth-century English version
of the original, both words and music, in Robert Edwards's
Commonplace-Book:

Into a mirthful May morning
As Phoebus did upspring
I saw a May both fair and gay,
Most goodly for to see.
I said to her,
Be kind
To me that was so pynd
For your love truly.

Transformations such as these show one of the effects of the
Reformation on court song. But in spite of such transformations and in spite of the reformers' suspicion both of the court-
song tradition and of the tradition of popular balladry and
seasonal festivities, both survived the Reformation, the former
only into the reign of James VI, the latter to be rediscovered
and transmuted in a later age. An important factor for continuity was Alexander Scott, the pre-Reformation author of
poems for music (which he may in some cases have composed
himself) who survived into the reign of James VI. Whatever
the vicissitudes of Scott's career and of the courtly tradition
during the turbulent period which preceded the young
James's re-establishment of the royal Court in Holyrood in
1579, both Scott and the courtly tradition managed to hang
on. Evidence for the continuity of *musik fyne* during the disturbed years is found in the collection of sacred and secular
part-song made by Thomas Wode between 1562 and 1590.

9

The fifth volume of Wode's collection includes items added by later hands as late as 1620; these include both words and music of Scott's fine poem 'Departe, departe', suggesting that it had enjoyed a continuous life from its composition in 1547. However, in this case it is clear that the music was fitted to the words after the words were written, for the poem in the Bannatyne manuscript opens

Departe, departe, departe,
Allace! I most departe . . .

while the words set under the music leave out one of the 'departes'—

Departe, departe,
Allace, I most departe . . .

so as to fit in with the music. Exactly how this court-poem became a court-song is a matter of conjecture: the interesting fact is that it continued to be remembered as a song throughout the reign of James VI and in the years after James's departure from Scotland when court-songs in Scots were no longer being written.

The arrival in Scotland from France in September 1579 of the young King James's charming and sophisticated kinsman Esmé Stuart, sixth Seigneur of Aubigny (whom the infatu-ated James created Duke of Lennox in 1581), led to a revival of the court culture that had been threatened and even forced out by reformers and politicians. The pastimes associated with Franco-Scottish culture re-emerged, to the grief and horror of the Kirk. 'Papists with great ruffes and syde bellies were suffered in the presence of the Kyng', was one complaint. And again: 'His Majesties chaste ears were frequently abused with unknown Italian and French forms of oaths, days were turned into nights, and Arran's mistress infected the air of the court.' However that may be, the fact that the Scots poet Alexander Montgomerie was one of Aubigny's company and was now brought into association with the King is much more relevant to our concerns. Montgomerie, then about thirty years of age, was already an accomplished poet, indeed the finest writing in Scotland at that time. Though brought up as a Calvinist, he had embraced Roman Catholicism either on a visit to Spain or under the influence of Catholic teachers elsewhere on the Continent. He thought of himself as part of a continuous poetic tradition stretching back into the Middle Ages. He was also a Court poet. He wrote two poems for royal entertainments after the King's entry into Edinburgh in August 1579, the first of which hails the thirteen-year-old monarch:

Haill bravest burgeon brekking to the rose
The due of grace thy leivis mot unclose
The stalk of treuth mot grant the nurishing
The air of faith support thy florishing.
Thy noble counsell, lyk trees about thy grace,
Mot plantit be ilk ane into his place,
Quhais ruiting sure and toppis reaching he
Mot brek the storme befor it come to the . . .

The poet combines compliment and advice, and we have seen that this is an old Scottish courtly tradition.

Montgomerie established himself as James's favourite poet at Court by a successful 'flyting' with a rival, Hume of Polwarth. Flyting, poetry of mutual abuse, was a kind of poetic jousting and an old Scottish tradition. It was done before the King and his Court, and Montgomerie flyted with Polwarth before James VI as Dunbar had flyted with Kennedy before James IV. It is not a very subtle kind of abuse:

Polwart, yee peip like a mouse amongst thornes;
Na cunning yee keipe; Polwart yee peip.
Ye look like a sheipe and yee had two hornes
Polwart yee peipe like a mouse amongst thornes . . .

But James liked it, and judged Montgomerie the winner. He also accepted Montgomerie as his tutor in poetry. The relationship was an attractive one, and just as in the Scottish courtly tradition a poet could both flatter and admonish his sovereign in the same poem, so King James could both compliment and reprove his teacher, as when he wrote his 'admonition to the Master poet to be warr of great bragging hereafter, lest he not only slander him self; bot also the whole professours of the art'. It opens:

> Give patient eare to sumething I man saye
> Beloved Saunders maistre of our art
> The mouse did helpe the lion on a daye
> So I protest ye take it in good part
> My admonition cumming from a hart
> That wishes well to you and all your craft
> Who woulde be sorie for to see you smart
> Thogh other poets trowes ye be gone daft.

Montgomerie's poetry was closely associated with music. Not only did he write court-songs in the Franco-Scottish tradition; even his elaborate allegorical poem in 113 cunningly shaped stanzas of fourteen lines each, *The Cherrie and the Slae,* was written to a tune known as 'The Banks of Helicon'. That tune had connections with dance, so that a poem which was long considered to be essentially a complex allegorical poem to be read and meditated in the study could have been both danced and sung.

King James was not a great poet, but he was a competent versifier and an apt pupil. In 1581, when he was fifteen, he wrote a poem entitled in the manuscript, 'Song. The First Verses that Ever the King Made'. Though entitled 'Song' there is no evidence that it was intended for singing or indeed that James had the same musical interests as his poetic tutor or his grandfather James V. His poem opens:

> Since thought is free, thinke what thou will
> O troubled hart to ease thy paine
> Thought unrevealed can do no evill

> Bot wordes past out, cummes not againe
> Be cairefull aye for to invent
> The waye to gett thy owen intent.

This interestingly reveals the young King's awareness of his need to step warily among conflicting forces out to get control over him. For the struggle for control over the King was not at an end. In the so-called 'Ruthven Raid' of August 1582 certain Protestant lords who deplored the influence on James of the Sire d'Aubigny banded together and seized the King, holding him in their power until his escape in 1583 to estab-lish himself for the first time as truly his own master. Aubigny, who had to flee to France after the Ruthven Raid, died in Paris two years later. Montgomerie was now attached directly to the King rather than (as had been the case earlier) through his association with Aubigny. In August 1583 Montgomerie was granted a royal pension derived from the revenues of the see of Glasgow. With Montgomerie to help him, the King now set himself to draw up a programme for a poetic renais-sance in Scotland. To this end he published in 1584 *Ane schort treatise: conteining some reulis and cautelis to be observit and eschewit in Scottish poesie.*

King James, as everyone knows, was a learned king. He had been well drilled in Latin by the great Scottish humanist George Buchanan as well as by other teachers, including Peter Young. 'They gar me speik Latin ar I could speik Scotis,' he once said, and he was fluent in French and Italian. In November 1583 he decided to bring some books from Stirling to Holyrood, and Peter Young made a list (which still exists) of what they were. The books include Daneau's *Geographia Poetica,* Ronsard's *La Franciade* and two volumes of his *Poemes,* and Du Bellay's *Musagnoemachie* and *L'Olive augmentée.* We know that in preparing his *Reulis and Cautelis* he drew also on Gascoigne's *Certayne Notes of Instruction Con-cerning the Making of Verse,* George Puttenham's *The Arte of English Poesie* and other sixteenth-century critical works.

James's intention was to build on the best available modern criticism.

James's aim was not only critical but consciously Scottish. Recent works on the subject, he wrote, were 'never one of thame written in our language. For albeit sindrie hes written of it in English, quhilk is lykest to our language yit we differ from thame in sindrie reulis of Poesie, as ye will find be experience'. Perhaps inevitably, this learned manifesto with its programme for a Scottish poetic renaissance, in the words of Dr James Craigie, 'tended to be purely mechanical and external'. What R. D. S. Jack has called 'an unhealthy obsession with virtuoso manneristic effects'[2] was encouraged by James's stress on rhetorical devices. But at least James's treatise did summon poets to put forth all their powers in creating a new Scottish poetic movement. Poets from France and England—Du Bartas, Du Bellay, Henry Constable—were invited to Scotland and a conscious attempt was made to re-establish Edinburgh as in the mainstream of European poetic culture. More important than his theoretical treatise was James's organising and patronising of his 'Castalian band' of poets. The resulting efflorescence of both poetry and song (in spite of the King's lesser interest in music) was accompanied by a revival of part-music in both the Chapel Royal and the sang schools of the burghs.

Though Montgomerie taught King James his poetic craft and was the leading Scottish poet of his day, his Catholicism and his support of the Catholic cause in a tricky political situation got him into trouble in Scotland. We do not know exactly how things happened, but he left Scotland in 1586 on some sort of commission from the King, perhaps deliberately sent out of the way by the wily monarch who was playing both ends against the middle in his attempt to secure for himself the throne of England on Queen Elizabeth's death. The ship on which he travelled was boarded by the English and Montgomerie was taken prisoner and imprisoned presumably in England: we do not know the precise nature of the charge, but he was perhaps engaged in piracy with the King's encouragement in a subtle ploy to keep in favour with Spain. He was set free after the execution of Mary Queen of Scots and the defeat of the Armada had made the English government less suspicious of plots, and he returned to Scotland in late 1589 or in 1590, but evidently not to regain his royal pension. He complained poetically to his royal master:

Help, Prince, to whom, on whom not, I complene
But on, not to, fals Fortun ay my fo
Quho but, not by, a resone reft me fro
Quho did, not does, yet suld my self sustene.
Of crymis, not cairs, since I haif kept me clene
I thole, not thanks, thame, sir, who served me so
Quha heght, not held, to me and mony mo
To help, not hurt, but hes not byding bene:
Sen will, not wit, too lait—whilk I lament—
Of sight, not service, shed me from your grace
With, not without, your warrand yit I went
In wryt, not words: the papers are in place.
Sen chance, not change, hes put me to this pane
Let richt, not reif, my pensioun bring agane.

But James now had other fish to fry, and Montgomerie remained out of favour, all the more so since he was now associated with elements opposed to the King and his policy. We need not follow his subsequent disturbed career, nor trace the moods of grief and disappointment reflected in poems he wrote, addressed obliquely to the King. Outlawed and in hiding, he died in 1598, and James's epitaph for the master poet who taught him his poetic craft and encouraged him in his desire to encourage a Scottish poetic renaissance shows his remorse and regret:

What drousie sleepe doth syle your eyes allace
Ye sacred brethren of Castalian band
And shall the prince of Poets in our land
Goe thus to grave unmurned in anie cace
No; whett your pens ye imps of heavenlie grace
And toone me up your sweete resounding strings
And mounte him so on your immortall wings
That ever he may live in everie place
Remember on Montgomeries flowand grace
His suggred stile his weightie words divine
And how he made the sacred Sisters nine
There montaine quitte to followe on his trace
   Though to his buriall was refused the bell
   The bell of fame, shall aye his praises knell.

'His suggred stile': James admired, and Montgomerie must
have taught him to admire, what one might call a courtly
craftsmanship. James had earlier written a sonnet 'painting
out the perfect Poet':

A ripe ingine, a quicke and walkened witt
With summaire raisons suddainlie applied
For everie purpose using raisons fitt
With skillfulness where learning may be spied
With pitthie wordes for to express you by it
His full intention in his propre leide
The propertie wherof well has he tryit
With memorie to keepe what he doth reide
With skillfulness and figures which proceede
From rhetorick, with everlasting fame
With others wondering preassing with all speede
For to attaine to merite such a name
   All these into the perfect Poet be
   Gods grante I may attaine the laurell tree.

Montgomerie did not learn from James; it was of course the
other way round. But other members of James's Castalian

Band did learn from him, or at least try to apply his precepts. John Stewart of Baldynnis, a younger man than Montgomerie who, unlike him, was not established by the time the King established his royal authority (Montgomerie was old enough to have some of his poems represented in Bannatyne's collection of 1568), tried deliberately to put James's programme into effect. He addressed the King in the introduction to his poems: 'Sir, haifing red your majesteis maist prudent precepts in the devyn art of poesie, I haif assayit my sempill spreit to becum your heines scholler'. As Dr Jack has pointed out, his 'abbregement' of Ariosto's *Orlando Furioso* was 'undertaken as part of James's plan for rendering great European master-pieces into Scots'.[3] It is indeed a remarkable performance, done with verve and skill and a conscious delight in poetic craftsmanship. It is a cunning re-ordering of themes found in Ariosto's poem, less free and wide ranging in implication than its model, with everything more explicitly woven together. It is difficult to illustrate these qualities in a short quotation, but at least the craftsmanlike courtliness of the language can be illustrated in the poem ('In toung Arabic Wretin' we are told) by Medoro addressed to the fountain by which he had made love to Angelica, found and read by Roland:

O herbis greine and prettie plants formois,
O limpid wattir springing suave and cleir,
O cave obscuir aggriabill to thois
Quho wold them cuile in thy fresche umber deir,
Quhair Angelique maist beutifful but peir
In vaine desyrd be uthers monie mo,
Oft nakit lay betwixt my armes heir.
I, Medor puir, quhom ye haif eisit so
May not requyt you moir, bot quhair I go
Your praise sall evir stedfastlie induir.
Lords, ladies, knychts and lustie luifers tho
And everie gentle hart I will procuir

To wiss you weill and frie of dainger suir.
Both sone and mone and nymphs you saif from tort
And nevir pastor with his troup injuir
Your verduir ritche, O seimlie fair resort.
  But ay about you birdis blythlie sing
  And unmolestit be your silver spring.

It is perhaps unfair to judge the whole of Baldynnis's version of Ariosto's poem by this inset piece, very much a set piece in the high courtly tradition, and there are other qualities to be found elsewhere in the poem; but at least we can see here a strain of high courtliness combined with a self-delighting craftsmanship that reflects a Renaissance tradition with roots in the courtly love tradition of the Middle Ages. We shall not again find in Scotland, either in an inset piece or elsewhere, an address to 'Lords, ladies, knychts and lustie luifers'. Throughout the poem we find Baldynnis consciously striving to implement the rhetorical precepts of his royal master. Here, for example, in the account of Roland's madness, he uses the rhetorical device of a series of parallel words in sequence known as 'underwriting':

He raifs, he rugs, he bruisis, breaks and ryfs
With hands, with feit, with nails and teith alway;
He byts, he stricks, he tumbls, he turns, he stryfs
He glaiks, he gaips, he girns, he glours, he dryfs
Throw moss and montane, forrest, firth and plaine,
The birds, the beists, the boyes, the men and wyfs
With bruit moir hiddeus from his trublit braine
Than force of fluidis hurlland in great raine.

Finally—for I must resist the temptation to quote Stewart of Baldynnis at length—here is a sonnet that James would have admired prodigiously:

Dull dolor dalie dois delyt destroy,
Will wantith wit waist worn with wickit wo,
Cair cankert causith confortles convoy,

Seveir sad sorrow scharplie schoris so,
My myrthles mynd may mervell monie mo;
Promp peirles proper plesand perill preclair,
Fair fremmit freind, firm fellest frownyng fo,
Ryche rubie rycht renownit royall rair,
Send succor soone so suadge sall sourest sair,
Grant grivous gronyng gratious guerdon guid,
For favor flowing from fresche faces fair
Restoris rychtlie restles rancor ruid,
Bot beutie breding bittir boudin baill
Dois dalie deedly dwynyng dartis daill.

This is a poem of high artifice addressed to the poet's royal
master in an appeal for help. He asks the 'Ryche rubie rycht
renownit royal rair' to 'Send succor soone' and 'Grant grivous
gronyng gratious guerdon guid'. There would soon be noone to whom a Scottish poet could appeal for 'gratious
guerdon guid' or indeed any one in Scotland who could use
the word 'guerdon' in a poem without making himself sound
slightly ridiculous. This last moment of high courtliness in
the language of Scottish poetry was high indeed: Dunbar
had addressed James IV as 'Schir' and when he paid him
compliments—'Bot ye sa gracious ar and meik'—the note of
irony is only half suppressed. But then Dunbar was not a
member of a Castalian band organised by the King himself
to improve the state of Scots poetry.

The poet who replaced Montgomerie in the King's favour
was William Fowler, who was born in 1562, son of a well-
to-do Edinburgh lawyer. He eagerly absorbed Italian influences and at the request of the King translated Petrarch's
Trionfi. He also arranged ceremonies and amusements for the
Court and wrote sonnets under Italian influence, a consciously courtly poet. Although he wrote with confidence
and craftsmanship in Scots, he realised fairly early in his
career that the future of patronage lay with England and he
left for England with King James in 1603 to take up a position

in the Queen's household. One can trace the increasing anglicisation of his language. His best known poem is the sonnet he wrote during a stay in Orkney, which is a courtly love poem with a difference, securely anchored in Scottish time and place:

Upon the utmost corners of the world
And on the borders of this massive round,
Quhaire faites and fortoune hither hes me harld,
I do deplore my greiffs upon this ground,
And seing roring seis from roks rebound
By ebbs and streames of contrair routing tyds
And Phebus chariot in there waves ly dround,
Quha equallye now night and day devyds.
I cal to mynde the storms my thoughts abyds,
Which ever wax and never dois decress,
For nights of dole dayes joys ay ever hyds
And in there vayle doith al my weill suppress:
So this I sie; quhaire ever I remove
I chainge bot sees, but can not change my love.

The sonnet is a skilful welding of the personal and the conventional: the last line is of course a version of the Horatian *Coelum non animum mutant qui trans mare currunt.*

I have not time to discuss other poets who formed part of the Castalian Band who moved around the King, exchanged verses with him, and sometimes wrote at his command. Robert Hudson produced his version of Du Bartas's *Judith* at the King's request: the epistle dedicatorie of his work, addressed to James, says that it was done 'At your owne commandement eterprised, corrected by your Maiest. owne hande, and dedicated to your owne Highenesse.' Poems commissioned by the King, poems written in playful competition with him, poems presented to him 'in propyne', as a present—this is surely court poetry and court patronage of a very intensive kind.

One of the younger Castalians who began as a court poet

but who abandoned the courtly for the religious muse was Alexander Hume, younger brother of the Hume of Polwarth whom Montgomerie defeated in a flyting contest. "In princes' Courts, in the houses of greate men," he wrote in his preface to his *Hymnes or Sacred Songs,* "and at the assemblies of yong gentilmen and yong damosels, the chief pastime is to sing prophane sonnets, and vaine ballatis of love, or to rehearse some fabulos faits of Palmerine, Amadis or such-like raveries." Religious poetry was not, of course, considered by the Castalian Band as outside their province: James himself produced poetic versions of Psalms and other parts of the Bible and Montgomerie's *The Cherrie and the Slae* is a religious allegory. But Hume, who became minister of Logie, near Stirling, considered sacred verse the enemy of profane court poetry, which he abandoned. His one great poem, however, combines quiet religious feeling with perfect command of tone and language to evoke the course of a summer's day. It is entitled 'Of the Day Estivall'. Its movement owes nothing to the sonnet or to other courtly forms, but is more reminiscent of some sung versions of the Psalms. It opens with an invoca-tion to light:

O perfite light, quilk schaid away
The darkness from the light,
And set a ruler ou'r the day,
And uther ou'r the night;

Thy glorie when the day foorth flies
Mair vively dois appeare,
Nor at midday unto our eyes,
The shining sun is cleare.

Hour by hour the poem takes us through the course of a summer's day in a Scottish rural scene. Here are the 42nd, 43rd and 44th stanzas:

Now noone is went, gaine is mid-day,
The heat dois slake at last,
The sunne descends downe west away,
Fra three of clock be past.

A little cule of braithing wind,
Now softly can arise,
The warks throw heate that lay behind,
Now men may enterprise.

Furth fairis the flocks to seeke their fude,
On everie hill and plaine,
Ilk labourer as he thinks gude,
Steppes to his turne againe.

Here is the poem's conclusion:

With bellie fow the beastes belive,
Are turned fra the corne,
Quhilk soberly they hameward drive,
With pipe and lilting horne.

Throw all the land great is the gild
Of rustik folks that crie,
Of bleiting sheepe fra they be fild
Of calves and routing ky.

All labourers drawes hame at even,
And can till uther say,
Thanks to the gracious God of heaven,
Quhilk send this summer day.

This is as far from the style of the other Castalians as it is from that of Dunbar. Its pastoral feeling is equally far removed from that of Allan Ramsay's *Gentle Shepherd,* Robert Fergusson's Scots pastorals, or Burns's 'Cotter's Saturday Night'. Between Hume and the Fergusson-Burns view of a pastoral scene Gray's 'Elegy' had intervened:

'Twas e'ening when the spreckled gowdspink sang,
Whan new fa'an dew in blobs o' chrystal hang;
Than Will and Sandie thought they'd wrought eneugh,
And loos'd their sair toil'd owsen frae the pleugh: . . .

That is Robert Fergusson, and it is from another world.

One other Scots poet of James's time in Scotland remains to be mentioned before we come to consider the effect of the removal of the Court from Scotland. That is Mark Alexander Boyd, the figure whom Agnes Mure Mackenzie called a Castalian ghost, for, though we have Latin verses of his, only one poem in Scots survives. It is one of the most famous sonnets in the language:

Fra banc to banc, fra wod to wod, I rin
Ourhailit with my feble fantasie,
Lyc til a leif that fallis from a trie
Or til a reid ourblawin with the wind.
Twa gods gyde me; the ane of tham is blind,
Ye, and a bairn brocht up in vanitie;
The nixt a wyf ingenrit of the se
And lichter nor a dauphin with hir fin.
Unhappie is the man for evirmaire
That teils the sand and sawis in the aire;
Bot twyse unhappier is he, I lairn,
That feidies in his hairt a mad desyre
And follows on a woman throw the fyre,
Led be a blind and teichit be a bairn.

A courtly love complaint? Yes, with its references to Cupid and Venus. But its tone is rather different from what one expects in courtly love complaints. The powerful last line balances the whole poem on the edge of despair. Yet, oddly enough, it is not wholly original. James taught the Castalians to draw freely on French and Italian poetry. Boyd must have had in mind Ronsard's first sonnet set memorably to music by Jannequin and adroitly rendered by Montgomerie—

'Wha wald behald him whom a god so grievis'. Ronsard kept revising this sonnet and his final version ends with these lines:

Et cognoistra que l'homme se deçoit
Quand plein d'erreur un aveugle il reçoit
Pour sa conduite, un enfant pour son maistre.

Boyd's line—'Led be a blind and teichit be a bairn'—makes the same point with greater power and succinctness.

Some of James's Castalian Band went south with him in 1603 to continue their career as court poets in England, becoming English Cavalier poets. Notable among these was Sir Robert Ayton, whose achievements in English verse have led him to be called 'the father of the Cavalier lyric'. He learned what was in a sense a new language. How close to the Court he was in Scotland before 1603 we do not know, but his early poetry reveals some of the literary habits encouraged by the King and popular among the Castalians, though most of it that survives does so in forms showing later anglicisation of spelling and usage. Here is the opening of an early Scots sonnet by Ayton:

Pamphilia hath a number of gud pairtes
Which comendatione to hir worth impairtes
But amongest all, in one sho doth excell,
That sho can paint inimitablie well: . . .

The sonnet is a satirical epigram on a lady who painted herself to try to appear more beautiful and shows little of the con‑ trived grace of his best later work in English. Perhaps the discipline of writing in an idiom distinct from his native speech was good for his art, or at least for his special kind of art. At any rate Ayton made the conscious choice to accom‑ pany James to England, serve the Court there and cultivate a courtly English poetic speech. When travelling south in 1603 he already showed what he could do in his poem on the River

Tweed—which divides Scotland from England—addressed to the King and expressing his feelings on his decision to migrate:

> Faire famous flood which some tyme did devyde
> But now conjoyns two Diadems in one
> Suspend thy pace and some more softly slyde
> Since wee have made thee Trinchman of our mone.
> And since non's left but thy report alone
> To show the world our captains last farewell
> That courtesye I knowe when we are gon
> Neptune thy lord may it perchance reveale
> And you againe the same will not conceale
> But straight proclaim't through all his bremish bounds
> Till his high tydes this flowing tydeings tell
> And soe will send them with his murmering sounds
> To that Religious place whose stately walls
> Does keepe the hart which all our harts inthralls.

There are no specifically Scots words here. The two words which may sound strange to our ears, 'Trinchman' and 'bremish', are literary English. 'Trinchman' is for 'truchman', a word found in Caxton, Gascoigne and elsewhere in late fifteenth-century and sixteenth-century literary English, and indeed used by King James himself, meaning 'interpreter' or 'spokesman' (it is derived from the Arabic and is akin to 'dragoman'). 'Bremish', meaning 'raging', is Spenserian.

As my concern is what happened in Scotland I do not propose to follow Ayton's career as an English Cavalier poet, although I might mention his fine poem addressed to the King on the death of his infant son, beginning

> Did you ever see the day
> When Blossomes fell in midst of May?
> Rather, did you ever see
> all the Blossomes on the Tree
> grow to ripe fruit? Some must fall.

Nature sayes so, though not all.
Though one be fallen we have store:
the Tree is fresh and may have more.

One hears Ben Jonson here, but nothing specifically Scottish. More to my purpose is a song entitled 'Old-Long-syne' found in Volume III of James Watson's *Choice Collection of Comic and Serious Scots Poems* (1711)—a collection I shall have much to say about in my next lecture—and credibly attributed to Ayton. This is how it goes

Should old Acquaintance be forgot,
  And never thought upon,
The Flames of Love extinguished,
  And freely past and gone?
Is thy kind Heart now grown so cold
  In that Loving Breast of thine,
That thou canst never once reflect
  On Old-long-syne?

And so on for five more stanzas, the last of which is

If e'er I have a House, my Dear,
That truly is call'd mine,
And can afford but Country Cheer,
Or ought that's good therein;
Tho' thou were Rebel to the King,
And beat with Wind and Rain,
Assure thyself of Welcome Love,
For Old-long-syne.

The movement reminds us of Lovelace:

Stone walls do not a prison make,
  Nor iron bars a cage;
Minds innocent and quiet take
  That for a mermitage;
If I have freedom in my love,
  And in my soul am free,

Angels alone, that soar above,
  Enjoy such liberty.

The song printed in Watson's collection clearly has its roots in the Cavalier version of the courtly tradition. Here is what has happened to it in Allan Ramsay's *Tea-Table Miscellany* of 1724:

Should auld acquaintance be forgot
  Tho' they return with scars?
These are the noble hero's lot,
  Obtain'd in glorious wars:
Welcome, my Varo, to my breast,
  Thy arms about me twine,
And make me once again as blest
  As I was lang syne.

Methinks around us on each bough,
  A thousand cupids play,
Whilst o'er the groves I walk with you,
  Each object makes me gay:
Since your return the sun and moon
  With brighter beams do shine;
Streams murmur soft notes while they run,
  As they did lang syne.

There are three more stanzas, of which this is the last:

The hero, pleas'd with the sweet aire,
  And signs of gen'rous love,
Which had been utter'd by the fair,
  Bow'd to the powers above:
Next day, with consent and glad haste,
  Th' approach'd the sacred shrine;
Where the good priest the couple blest,
  And put them out of pine.

To anticipate the argument of my second lecture, I shall only say now that the movement from the courtly to the genteel is complete—or, to be more precise, the movement away from Scottish courtly to English courtly and thence to the genteel.

The fate of this song is indeed interesting. There were versions between Ayton's (if it *was* his) and Ramsay's: Henley and Henderson, in their centenary edition of Burns, quote from a unique broadside entitled 'An Excellent and proper new ballad, entitled *Old Lang Syne*, newly corrected and amended, with a large and new edition of several excellent love lines.' This is the text Watson used, except that he omitted the refrain:

On old long syne
On old long syne, my jo,
On old long syne:
That thou canst never once reflect
  On old long syne.

It looks as though the cavalier love song had been assimilated at least in part to the folk tradition before re-emerging in its 'improved' genteel version. Of course we all know what Burns made of it. He produced several versions, the first in a letter to Mrs Dunlop dated 7 December 1788 (where the chorus is

For auld lang syne, my jo,
  For auld lang syne;
Let's hae a waught o' Malaga
  For auld lang syne.)

It includes, as all his versions do, the two moving stanzas about the boys running about the braes and paidling in the burn, which to my mind are clearly Burns's own, although he never claimed the poem as his at all. 'Light be the turf on the breast of the heaven-inspired Poet who composed this glorious Fragment!' he commented to Mrs Dunlop. And in writing to George Thomson in 1793 enclosing a slightly different version he remarked: '. . . the following song, the old song of the olden times, and which has never been in print, nor even in manuscript, untill I took it down from an old man's singing; is enough to recommend any air.' Whatever the precise part Burns played in creating the song he delivered to Mrs Dunlop and to George Thomson (he provided yet a third version in his interleaved copy of the Scots Musical Museum, with the comment that this version was 'The original and by much the best set of the words of this song') he was clearly responsible for placing it firmly in the folk tradition. The courtly, the genteel, and the folk: we have here a history in miniature of one aspect of the Scottish poetic tradition.

But I am anticipating, led away by the attribution of Watson's 'Old-long-syne' to Ayton. Let me return to Scotland after the departure of the King and his Court in 1603. Some of the court songs survived throughout the seventeenth century, especially in Aberdeen, where Alexander Scott's courtly part-song 'O lustie May' was transcribed with all its musical parts by David Melvill at the end of his *Book of Roundells* in 1604 and where in the 1660s John Forbes produced his famous cantus part-book, *Songs and Fancies*. But with no Court or royal patronage no new poetry or music in the courtly style was produced: part-song gave way to monophonic song and in some cases simplified versions of both words and music entered into the popular tradition. Poets themselves turned to popular folk airs or dance tunes (some of which in turn may have derived from more sophisticated courtly forms) to match words to them.

The loss of court patronage for Scots poets and the move from Scots to English by Ayton and others was one of several factors making for the decline of the Scots language as a literary medium. Historically, the language we call Scots was a development of the Anglian speech of the Northumbrians who established their kingdom of Bernicia as far north as the Firth of Forth in the seventh century. This northern Anglo-Saxon language flourished in Lowland Scotland and emerged into a distinct language on its own, capable of rich expansion by borrowing from Latin, French and other sources with its own grammatical forms and methods of borrowing. By the time of the Makars of the fifteenth century it was a highly sophisticated poetic language, based on the spoken speech of the people but enriched by many kinds of expansion, invention and 'aureation'. Distinct from literary English, but having much in common with it, literary Scots took its place in the late Middle Ages as one of the great literary languages of Europe. At the same time it was vulnerable to displacement by English, especially when the prestige of English poets was high. Religious and political factors increased that vulnerability. The consequences of the Reformation Parliament of 1560 were that the reformers were drawn closer to Protestant England and away from Scotland's traditional ally France, which remained Catholic. Politico-religious disputes in sixteenth-century Scotland thus made for a strong English influence on Protestant Scotland. The translation of the Bible in use by Scottish Protestants, first the Geneva Bible and then the Authorised or King James Bible, made a somewhat old-fashioned English the language of prayer and edification in Scotland even when the ordinary spoken language remained Scots. The removal of the Court in 1603 and the association of all courtliness of language henceforth with an English Court was yet another factor depressing literary Scots.

There are many paradoxes here. If Protestant Scotland looked to England it was at the same time true that the revolt of the Covenanters against royal authority in the seventeenth century was in a sense an expression of national Scottish feeling and that what might be called the evangelical side of Scottish Protestantism often expressed strong national sentiment, and this remained true as late as 1843, when the Disruption was seen as an assertion of national dignity as well as of ecclesiastical independence. Again, if Presbyterian Scotland looked to England, it might be assumed that the royalist Cavalier tradition in Scotland, which was Episcopalian or even Catholic in religious sentiment where it was not wholly

secular, would cultivate a more purely Scottish set of sentiments. In a sense this is what happened in the late seventeenth
and the eighteenth centuries, after the ousting of James VII
of Scotland and II of England and the emergence of a Jacobite
movement dedicated to the restoration of the exiled House of
Stewart. Jacobite sentiment, especially in Aberdeen and the
north-east of Scotland, tended to be Episcopalian and, as
such, had a sense of continuity with older Scottish traditions
of poetry and music that the Covenanting tradition did not
have. But this is to look forward into the eighteenth century.
In the seventeenth century, in the decades after the removal of
the Court from Scotland, the Cavalier tradition emerged as
wholly English and there was nothing in Scottish life or
thought that encouraged a Cavalier tradition expressing itself
in Scots, although there were a few poets in Scotland who
grew up after James's departure but remembered and in some
degree imitated the old Scots courtly tradition—Sir William
Mure of Rowallan, for example. It might be said that the only
true Scottish Cavalier who remained in Scotland was James
Graham, fifth Earl and first Marquis of Montrose. Montrose's
handful of poems are all in English, though there are sugges-
tions of Scots in a minor piece, his 'Lynes on the Killing of
the Yearle of Newcastell's Sonne's Doge'. Here are the
opening two stanzas of a poem he set to the tune of an existing
song entitled 'I'll never love thee more':

My dear and only Love, I pray
  This noble World of thee,
Be govern'd by no other Sway
  But purest Monarchie.
For if Confusion have a Part,
  Which vertuous Souls abhore,
And hold a Synod in thy Heart,
  I'll never love thee more.

> Like *Alexander* I will reign
> And I will reign alone,
> My thoughts shall evermore disdain
> A Rival on my Throne.
> He either fears his Fate too much,
> Or his Deserts are small,
> That puts it not unto the Touch,
> To win or lose it all.

The last four lines of the second stanza are often quoted for their sentiment without any consideration of the fact that they belong to a sophisticated court song in which the author plays ironically with the controversial items in politics and religion that were dividing both Scotland and England at the time it was written. There is nothing that sounds particularly Scots in the poem, any more than there is in the powerful eight-line poem he wrote on the execution of King Charles I, beginning

> Great, Good and Just, could I but rate
> My Grief to Thy too Rigid Fate!
> I'd weep the World in such a Strain,
> As it would once deluge again: . . .

But the lines he wrote on the eve of his own execution do show something characteristically Scots. It is only a single word, the Scots word 'Airth' (direction), but it is strategically placed in a powerful position in the opening line:

> Let them bestow on ev'ry Airth a Limb;
> Open all my Veins, that I may swim
> To Thee my Saviour, in that Crimson Lake;
> Then place my pur-boil'd Head upon a Stake;
> Scatter my Ashes, throw them in the Air:
> Lord (since Thou know'st where all these Atoms are)
> I'm hopeful, once Thou'lt recollect my Dust,
> And confident Thou'lt raise me with the Just.

With that poem, it might be said, the courtly tradition in

Scots poetry died. Yet it is very different from the older Court poetry. It is religious, in a grim and confident way, with no play in it. It was difficult to be playful amid the bitter civil conflicts of seventeenth-century Scotland.

Yet we are never done with paradoxes. William Cleland fought as a young officer with the Covenanters, and after his death in 1689 at the battle of Dunkeld at the age of twenty-eight a collection of his poems was published. One of these was written when Cleland was an eighteen-year-old student at the College of Edinburgh. It is a song, written to a traditional tune known as 'Hullo my fancy', a strange composition to come from an ardent young Covenanter. It is entirely in English, and it is totally un-courtly. Here are two verses, as printed in Watson's collection in 1706:

What multitude of Notions
    doth disturb my Pate,
Considering the Motions.
How th' Heav'ns are preserved
And this World served,
    In Moisture, Light and Heat!
If one Spirit sits the outmost Circle turning,
Or one turns another continuing in journeying,
If Rapid circles Motion be that which they call burning!
    Hallow my Fancie, whither wilt thou go?

Fain also would I prove this,
    by considering,
What that, which you call Love is:
Whether it be a Folly,
Or a Melancholy,
    Or some Heroick thing!
Fain I'd have it prov'd, by one whom Love hath wounded
And fully upon one his desire hath founded,
Whom nothing else could please tho' the
                   World were rounded!
    Hallow my Fancie, whither wilt thou go?

Montrose and Cleland, the sombre Cavalier and the sprightly Covenanter—there does indeed seem to be a confusion of categories. Both write in English, and the significance of that is at least clear. One concludes a tradition and the other makes contact with an older song tradition in a rather wildly individual way. Neither represents the road Scottish poetry was to take. For the real and lasting consequences to Scottish literature of the removal of the Court in 1603 we must look elsewhere.

NOTES

1. Helena Mennie Shire, *Song Dance and Poetry of the Court of Scotland under King James VI,* Cambridge, 1969, pp.6-7. I am indebted to Mrs Shire throughout this chapter.
2. R. D. S. Jack, Ed., *A Choice of Scottish Verse 1560-1660,* London, 1978, p.13.
3. *Ibid.,* p.21.

II

THE EMERGENCE OF GENTILITY

In 1706, the year before the 'incorporating union' between Scotland and England was finally effected, the Edinburgh printer James Watson produced the first of his three-volume collection entitled *A Choice Collection of Comic and Serious Scots Poems*. As an attempt to bring together elements that could provide continuity in a Scottish poetic tradition it is a very curious selection, but as an indication of what seemed available at the beginning of the eighteenth century it is illuminating. The volume opens with 'Christ's Kirk on the Green', 'Composed (as was supposed) by King James the Fifth'. Whether it was really by James V, or by James I as the Bannatyne Manuscript says, or by neither of these, is not a question relevant to my purpose. What *is* relevant is that this is a poem descriptive of popular revelry written in an artful ten-line stanza which in fact Watson's version simplifies into nine lines as it also somewhat modernises the language. James Kinsley has written that 'the poem dances lightly on in the measure and with the artless clarity of folk-song',[1] while Allan Maclune has expressed the view that 'the intricacy of the metrical form alone precludes the probability of a folk origin'[2] and I am inclined to agree with the latter view. It certainly required considerable poetic craftsmanship to imitate the stanza successfully in the eighteenth century, as Robert Fergusson and Robert Burns were to do. But whoever the author was, and wherever he derived his skill, he produced a poem celebrating revelry in an atmosphere reminiscent of that pre-Reformation kind of seasonal or festive celebration that the Town Council of Edinburgh after the Reformation did their best to stamp out. To Watson, who was an ardent Scottish patriot who had suffered imprisonment for printing a pamphlet attacking the betrayal by the Government of the Scottish people in their sabotaging of the Scottish trading company that tried to colonise the Isthmus of Darien, who also had Jacobite leanings and was clearly nostalgic for a lost phase of Scottish culture, this poem must have evoked a lost Scotland he would like to commemorate if not to revive.

The other nineteen poems in Watson's volume of 1706 are strangely assorted. They include a seventeenth-century poem of popular revelry, much more clearly in the folk tradition than 'Christ's Kirk on the Green', entitled 'The Blythsome Wedding' (titled in other texts 'The Blythsome Bridal') sometimes attributed to Francis Sempill; some miscellaneous and minor seventeenth-century occasional and satirical pieces mostly in English and occasionally in an anglicised Scots, six poems by Montgomerie, including all 114 stanzas of *The Cherry and the Slae* in a somewhat modernised spelling; the comic dog-Latin (or Latin-Scots) *Polemo-Middinia* attributed to Drummond of Hawthornden; and William Cleland's 'Hallow my Fancie'.

Among the group I have described as miscellaneous seventeenth-century poems is one entitled 'The Life and Death of the Piper of Kilbarchan or, The Epitaph of Habbie Simson'. It is by Robert Sempill of Beltress (*c.* 1595–1668) who belonged to a family of versifiers, and it laments, half-seriously and half-humorously, the death of the piper of the village of Kilbarchan in Renfrewshire and the loss of all the mirthful and celebratory activities that he and his piping encouraged. Sempill was a landed gentleman, so his celebration of rustic merriment might be considered to have something of condescending patronage about it. And indeed, the humorous note that emerges in the description of these festivities might be interpreted as somewhat condescending. David Craig says that it 'gives the effect, though written by a

landed gentleman, of sharing directly and artlessly in a village
life whose high moments were signalled by music',[3] but I am
not sure about this direct and artless sharing. The writer is
amused by what he describes, and he writes in a Scots which
is no longer a literary language but a vernacular that a writer
would only use when deliberately trying to imitate popular
speech. Here is how it opens (not precisely in Watson's text,
which has some obvious errors, but in his text as corrected by
R. D. S. Jack from broadside versions of 1689):

> Kilbarchan now may say, alas!
> For she has lost her game and grace,
> Both 'Trixie' and 'The Maiden Trace';
> But what remead?
> For no man can supply his place,
> Hab Simson's dead.
>
> Now who shall play 'The Day it Daws'?
> Or 'Hunts Up', when the cock he craws?
> Or who can for our Kirk-town-cause
> Stand us in stead?
> On bagpipes (now) no body blaws,
> Sen Habbie's dead.
>
> Or wha will cause our shearers shear?
> Wha will bend up 'The Brags of Weir',
> Bring in the bells or good play meir,
> In time of need?
> Hab Simson cou'd, what needs you speer?
> But (now) he's dead.

The stanza will be familiar to all who know Burns and even
more so to those who know also Allan Ramsay and Robert
Fergusson. It has a long history going back to the twelfth-
century troubadours, and it had been much used in Scots
poetry before Sempill of Beltrees. It was also to be so much
used by imitators of Sempill's poem that already in the early

eighteenth century Allan Ramsay was dubbing it 'Standart Habby' to indicate that it had become a standard stanza in Scottish poetry.

The references in Sempill's poem are to folk festivities and folk tunes, and it would take a whole lecture to unravel the references and allusions (as Kenneth Buthlay did in a recent article).[4] The poem is meant to sound as though it comes from the people, and it depends on a knowledge of popular customs and festivities for its effectiveness if not for its intelligibility. At the same time this is a *mock* elegy, not a serious lament, and the father of a host of mock elegies in Scottish poetry reaching to Burns's 'Poor Maillie's Elegy'. Though it is written in a popular Scots speech, it draws on English pronunciation when that is convenient, so that 'dead' is pronounced in the Scots way, 'deid', in the first stanza, rhyming with 'remead' (remedy), 'dead' in the second stanza (rhyming with 'stead'), and 'deid' again in the third stanza (rhyming with 'need'). This, incidentally, was to be a feature of the poetry of both Fergusson and Burns and added to the flexibility of their poetic language, which could draw on the resources of both Scots and English. At the same time, it might be said that Sempill's kind of verse lacks a dimension. With the sound of the first three stanzas of 'Habbie Simson' still (I hope) in your ears, listen to two stanzas in almost the same form (Scott's stanza has one more line) from a poem in the Bannatyne MS by Alexander Scott. It is a love lament written in the old courtly tradition: these are the sixth and seventh stanzas:

> I may persaif that weill be thiss
> That all the blythnes, joy, and bliss,
> The lusty, wantoun lyf, I wiss,
> >   Of lufe is hyne;
> And no remeid, sen so it iss,
> Bot paciens, suppoiss I muss
> >   That suld be myne.

For nobillis hes nocht ay renown,
Nor gentillis ay the gayest goun,
They carry victuallis to the toun
    That werst dois dyne:
Sa blissely to busk I boun,
Ane uthir eitis the berry doun
    That suld be myne.

The eight stanzas of this poem all end in the line 'That suld be myne' or some slight variant of it, which puts considerable strain on the rhyming, as do the five rhyming lines (as opposed to the four rhyming lines of the Habbie Simson form of the stanza) in each stanza. I have chosen these two stanzas not, however, because of their technical skill but because they share some features with 'Habbie Simson' and so make the difference between the two poems all the clearer. Scott has 'and no remeid' as Sempill has 'But what remead?' (the phrase is to go on and on in Scottish poetry). More signifi- cantly, Scott, in spite of his artful, courtly style, draws on popular proverbial expressions. Listen again to the second of the stanzas I quoted:

For nobillis hes nocht ay renown,
Nor gentillis ay the gayest goun,
They cary victuallis to the toun
    That werst dois dyne:
Sa blissely to busk I boun,
Ane uthir eitis the berry doun
    That suld be myne.

They carry victuals to the town who dine worst. Though I get to the bush, another eats the berry that should be mine. Homely expressions, with a ring of a country proverb, yet not expressed in a homely fashion. They take their place in care- fully weighted verse without any sense of strain. Scott can move freely from the spoken language on which his literary language is ultimately based to his refined poetic speech, the

two elements continually reflecting on each other and enriching each other. That is what happens when there is a flourish-
ing literary language in continuous relationship with the
daily spoken language, however much it may on occasion
transcend it. By Sempill's day the literary language of Scottish
poetry, if it was at all ambitious and aimed high, was English,
and Scots was coming more and more to be used in patronising, nostalgic, antiquarian, jocular, rustic or 'low life' poems.
So Sempill's 'Habbie Simson' is important historically, both
for drawing attention to the possibilities of folk-humour as a
way of bringing the vernacular into current poetry and for
reviving a stanza form that was to play an important part in
eighteenth-century Scottish poetry. But at the same time it
illustrates the loss of a dimension in the language and range of
reference of Scots poetry. The real question now was whether
that dimension could be restored by writing Scottish poetry
in English.

The second and third volumes of Watson's collection, published in 1709 and 1711 respectively, do not give us much help
in answering this question. Volume II opens with a doggerel
poem in couplets 'Robert III of Scotland's answer to Henry IV
of England', attributed in the Maitland Folio MS, from which
Watson transcribed it, to 'Deine David Steil'. It was popular
as a broadside, but it had nothing to offer to Scottish poetry at
the beginning of the eighteenth century. More interesting are
two poems that follow, both by John Burel, an Edinburgh
goldsmith who tried his hand at courtly ceremonial verse and
succeeded in suggesting a kind of middle-class matter-of-
factness that is very different from anything in Scott or
Drummond:

> At Edinburgh, as micht be seene,
> Upon the nintene day of Maj,
> Our Princes Spous, and soveraigne Queen,
> Hir nobil entry maid that day,
> Maist honorable, was hir convoy,
> With gladnes gret, triumph and joy.

This is the first stanza of a poem celebrating James VI's Queen's entry into Edinburgh on 19 May 1590, and if you put it beside Alexander Scott's celebration of Queen Mary's entry into Edinburgh in 1561, which I quoted in my first lecture, you can see the decline in verbal polish. Watson follows this with another poem by Burel, 'The Passage of the Pilgremer', a long visionary poem in the stanza of Montgomerie's *The Cherry and the Slae* probably influenced by Montgomerie's poem: it too simplifies the courtliness of speech associated with this kind of writing, but not crudely, and it brings in classical names in a direct matter-of-fact way that is rather attractive, as is the engaging description of animals. It might be argued that this sort of use of an older Scottish stanza helped to accommodate it to the kind of use that Burns was to make of it.

The next poem in Watson's second volume is a mock-epitaph in the Habbie Simson tradition by William Lithgow, followed by a poem by Sir George Mackenzie modelled entirely on the style of late seventeenth-century English poetry:

I sing no Triumphs, nor such empty Things,
'Tis Solid *Friendship* gives me Theme and Wings:
Friendship! that wiser Rival of Vain Love,
Which does more Firm, tho' not so Fiery prove; . . .

Sir George Mackenzie—'the Bluidy Mackenzie' of Covenanting tradition—was Lord Advocate under both Charles II and James VII, a man of cosmopolitan culture, founder of the Advocates Library (now the National Library of Scotland) and writer of works of political philosophy, history and fiction. For him clearly English was the proper literary language for an educated Scot. Watson follows Mackenzie's poem by another in English, Drummond's 'Forth Feasting' and the volume concludes, as though in despair in finding anything suitable written in Scots, with three short poems by Sir Robert Ayton.

Watson's third volume, which appeared in 1711, opens

with 'The Flyting betwixt Polwart and Montgomery', thus beginning vigorously in an old Scottish poetic tradition. There follow eight poems by Ayton, and then comes 'The Country Wedding', a sixteenth-century poem of rustic celebration that has obviously been through simplification and modernisation in broadside versions:

> *Rob's Jock* came to wooe our *Jennie*
> On a Feast Day when he was fow;
> She busked her and her bonnie
> When she heard *Jock* was come to wooe: . . .

Simple stuff, with a folk feeling to it, a feeling recaptured often in later Scottish song and captured by Burns in the opening of 'Duncan Gray':

> Duncan Gray cam here to woo,
>   Ha, ha, the wooing o't,
> On blythe Yule night when we were fu', . . .

Other poems in Watson's third volume include a number of trivial pieces in rather stiff English, 'Old-Long-Syne', which I discussed in my first lecture, some student poems and songs in Latin and Latin-English and seven poems by Montrose. There is also the song Watson entitles 'Lady Anne Bothwell's Balow', a lullaby sung to her child by a girl (said to be Anne Bothwell, daughter of a Bishop of Orkney) deserted by a lover whose father the child is. This is a folk theme that attracted the attention of Scottish Cavalier poets, who handled it in English in a variety of versions. Watson's version is in English, but in spite of a certain courtliness of speech the undertones of a vernacular folk utterance are audible:

> *Balow* my Boy, ly still and sleep,
> It grieves me sore to hear thee weep;
> If thou'll be silent, I'll be glad,
> Thy Mourning makes my Heart full sad:
> *Balow* my Boy, thy Mother's Joy,
> Thy Father's bred me great Annoy.

It goes to an old tune—monophonic, not part-song—to which words first appeared in *The Gude and Godlie Ballatis* of 1568.

Watson's *Choice Collection* was intended as a patriotic assertion of Scotland's poetic heritage in the face of the loss of political identity involved in the Union of 1707. His preface makes this abundantly clear:

> As the frequency of Publishing Collections of Miscellaneous Poems in our Neighbouring Kingdoms and States, may, in a great measure, justify an Undertaking of this kind with us; so 'tis hoped, that this being the first of its Nature which has been publish'd in our own Native *Scots* Dialect, the Candid Reader may be the more easily induced, though the Consideration thereof to give some Charitable Grains of Allowance, if the Performance come not up to such a Point of Exactness as may please an over nice Palate . . .

Watson is not apologising for the quality of the poems, but for the lack of 'exactness' in his performance as an anthologist. At the same time, there is a defensive note in his reference to 'our own Native *Scots* Dialect', suggesting an awareness that perhaps its day as a poetic medium is done. Further, although the majority of the poems in the first volume are in Scots, there is an increasing proportion of pieces in English in the subsequent volumes: in the third volume they far outnumber the pieces in Scots. As a basis on which to build a new Scottish poetry Watson's *Collection* was decidedly shaky. The fact that it ignored completely the great poetry of the fifteenth-century makars is understandable in the light of the unavailability of texts and the change in the language which made Henryson and Dunbar not easily intelligible to eighteenth-century Scottish readers even though they spoke a version of Scots themselves. Watson ignored ballads, too, which is perhaps surprising in view of the great interest in ballads that was about to spring up. There are also surprisingly few song lyrics. Perhaps Watson's most important achievement so far as later Scottish poets were concerned was to make one aspect of the achievement of the makars available through printing so much of Montgomerie and to perpetuate both the older and the newer tradition of poetry of popular revelry by printing both 'Christ's Kirk on the Green' and 'Habbie Simson'.

Watson printed the best texts available to him, though these were often poor broadsides. Popularity in broadsides at least indicates continuing vitality, so for the most part what Watson printed, curiously assorted though it may seem to us, represented what appeared to be available as poetic currency in the Scotland of his day. It is clear from Watson and from many other indications that throughout the seventeenth century the line between folk-song and 'art' poem was often obscured in Scotland; courtly poems found their way to popular singers and printers of broadsides, as well as to private collectors; and changes, corruptions, emendations and additions were the natural result. The loss of a courtly tradition of artfulness and elegance made it easier for such changes to take place. Awareness of that loss, not always on a fully conscious level, led to the search for other kinds of artfulness and elegance. And that is where gentility comes in.

Allan Ramsay left his native Leadhills in Lanarkshire about 1700 to settle in Edinburgh where, on 12 May 1712 he together with a number of other young men founded the Easy Club 'in order that by a Mutual improvement in Conversation they may become more adapted for fellowship with the politer part of mankind and Learn also from one another's happy observation'. All members of the club adopted pseudonyms. Ramsay adopted that of Isaac Bickerstaff, a fictitious character invented by Swift and used afterwards facetiously by other of the Queen Anne Wits. In 1713 the Club decided to adopt Scottish names and Ramsay changed from Isaac Bickerstaff to Gavin Douglas. The year before the Club 'ordered that one Specktator be Read at every meeting till all be read' with Ramsay providing the first volume. The Club survived until late in 1715, and it has been surmised that it was suppressed after the Jacobite rising of 1715 because of its Jacobite sympathies.

Emulation of the Queen Anne Wits and a harking back to the old Scottish makars; desire for 'a Mutual improvement in Conversation' and suspected Jacobitism: training to be English gentlemen and proud to be Scottish patriots—we can see these apparently conflicting aims in the Easy Club as we see them in the life and work of Ramsay himself. I cannot here attempt to give any account of Ramsay's career as poet, editor, reviser, populariser, experimenter, clubman, satirist, champion of the theatre, patriot, would-be wit, *entrepreneur* and general busybody. But it is safe to say that all his multifarious activities add up to a vivid illustration of the problems arising from a lack of cultural authority and of artistic patronage of the kind that had once been provided by the Court. It is easy to say that the folk tradition replaced the lost court tradition and that Ramsay's interest in collecting folk songs, in which he was followed by so many eighteenth-century poets, editors and collectors, illustrates this. But the situation is more complicated than this. Some folk songs had courtly origins; some had themes in common with court song; some were deliberately 'unfolked' by being cast in a mould of neo-classic gentility. This last phrase requires some explanation.

Some examples will help to explain. The great eighteenth-century collector of Scottish songs (the words only), David Herd, whose two volumes of *Ancient and Modern Scottish Songs* published in 1776 conscientiously prints whatever he could find of remaining Scottish folk songs, however fragmentary or in whatever state, exactly as he found them, printed a song called 'Wallifou fa' the Cat' which went to the old tune of 'Tweedside'. Here is its opening stanza:

> There was a bonnie wi' laddie,
>   Was keeping a bonny whine sheep;
> There was a bonnie wee lassie,
>   Was wading the water sae deep,

Was wading the water sae deep,
  And a little above her knee;
The laddie cries unto the lassie,
  Come down Tweedside to me.

In Allan Ramsay's collection of songs Scots and English both old, altered, and wholly original, first published in 1724 and entitled *The Tea-Table Miscellany,* we find a song entitled 'Tweed-Side' which goes to the same tune. Here is how it opens:

What beauties does Flora disclose?
  How sweet are her smiles upon Tweed?
Yet Mary's still sweeter than those;
  Both nature and fancy exceed.
Nor daisy, nor sweet-blushing rose,
  Not all the gay flow'rs of the field,
Not Tweed gliding gently through those,
  Such beauty and pleasure does yield.

Many of the songs in *The Tea-Table Miscellany* are old songs printed as Ramsay found them. He tells us that he marked them with a 'Z'. Here is one, entitled 'Maggie's Tocher' (Dowry) subtitled 'To its ain tune':

The meal was dear short syne,
  We muckl'd us a' the gither;
And Maggie was in her prime,
  When Willie made courtship till her:
Twa pistols charg'd beguess,
  To gie the courting shot;
And syne came ben the lass
  Wi' swats drawn frae the but.
He first speer'd at the guidman,
  And syne at Giles the mither,
An ye wad gi's a bit land,
  We'd buckle us e'en the gither.

And so on, for six more verses.

The more we study *The Tea-Table Miscellany* the more
miscellaneous it appears. Montrose's 'My dear and only love,
I pray' is here, with no indication of its authorship. It follows
immediately on 'The auld Wife beyont the Fire' which opens:

There was a wife won'd in a glen,
 And she had dochters nine or ten,
That sought the house baith but and ben,
 To find their mam a snishing.
  The auld wife beyont the fire,
  The auld wife aniest the fire,
  The auld wife aboon the fire,
  She died for lack of snishing.

There are many such poems with the genuine folk ring: 'Fy
gar rub her o'er wi' Strae', 'My Jo Janet', 'The Mill, Mill-O',
'Steer her up, and had her gawn', 'Todlen butt, todlen ben',
which Burns called 'perhaps the finest bottle-song that ever
was composed', and scores more. There are also many songs
written by Ramsay or his friends to old airs; some keep part of
the original, some change them totally. Ramsay also wrote
songs in Scots in the folk tradition, like his lively drinking
song in roaring Scots 'Up in the Air'. The refrain of this is
old, and perhaps some other lines are too, but Ramsay has got
into the spirit of the original magnificently:

Now the Sun's gane out of Sight,
Beet the Ingle, and snuff the Light:
In Glens the Fairies skip and dance,
And Witches wallop o'er to *France*,
   Up in the Air
   On my bonny grey Mare.
And I see her yet, and I see her yet,
   Up in, &c.

It is the genteel versions of older songs or new genteel words
to older folk words that are most relevant to the points I am
trying to make. Here, for example, is one of several songs

written to the old folk tune, 'The Broom of Cowdenknows':

> Teach me, Chloe, how to prove
>   My boasted flame sincere;
> 'Tis hard to tell how dear I live,
>   And hard to hide my care.

English as well as Scots folk songs are re-done in this way. Here is the opening of a song written to the old tune, 'Black-ey'd Susan':

> Ye powers! was Damon then so blest,
>   To fall to charming Delia's share;
> Delia, the beauteous maid, possest
>   Of all that's soft, and all that's fair?

There is every kind of mixture between the folk and what I have called the genteel. To the tune of 'The Gallant Shoe-maker' there is a poem entitled 'Celia's Reflections on herself for fighting Philander's Love'. This is, in some degree, in the Scots vernacular, but its tone suggests polite sophistication:

> Young Philander woo'd me lang,
>   But I was peevish and forbad him,
> I wadna tent his loving sang;
>   But now I wish, I wish I had him:
> Ilk morning when I view my glass,
>   Then I perceive my beauty going;
> And when the wrinkles seize the face,
>   Then we may bid adieu to wooing.
>
> My beauty, anes so much admir'd,
>   I find it fading fast, and flying,
> My cheeks, which coral-like appear'd,
>   Grow pale, the broken blood decaying.
> Ah! we may see ourselves to be,
>   Like summer-fruit that is unshaken;
> When ripe, they soon fall down and die,
>   And by corruption quickly taken.

The Scots here is not, of course, the full-blooded Scots of the older Scottish poets, but a sprinkling to give a Scottish flavour to a neo-classic English. This use of Scots is very different from the vivid Scots of Ramsay's own poems of Edinburgh low-life such as the elegies on Maggie Johnston, John Cowper and Lucky Wood, in the Habby Simson tradition but given new vigour and rooted in an urban rather than than a rural environment. The use of sprinkled Scots is common not only in the songs of *The Tea-Table Miscellany* but throughout Scottish song of the eighteenth century. Very often a theme derived from English song has been given a Scottish coloration by such a sprinkling. This is not a use of Scots as a confident poetic language of its own.

Ramsay's 'pastoral comedy', *The Gentle Shepherd*, illustrates very interestingly some of the aspects of literary language that Scottish poets were having to grapple with in the early eighteenth century. The dedication, to the Countess of Eglintoun, is in a consciously elegant English:

> The love of approbation, and a desire to please the best, have ever encouraged the poets to finish their designs with cheerfulness. But, conscious of their own ability to oppose a storm of spleen and haughty ill-nature, it is generally an ingenious custom among them to chuse some honourable shade.
>
> Wherefore I beg leave to put my Pastoral under your Ladyship's protection. If my Patroness says the shepherds speak as they ought, and that there are several natural flowers that beautify the rural wild, I shall have good reason to think myself safe from the awkward censure of some pretending judges that condemn before examination . . .

William Hamilton of Bangour wrote a verse dedication to add to Ramsay's prose one, in similarly elegant English. It begins:

Accept, O Eglintoun, the rural lays,
That, bound to thee, thy poet humbly pays:
The muse that oft has rais'd her tuneful strains,
A frequent guest on Scotia's blissful plains;
That oft has sung, her list'ning youth to move,
The charms of beauty, and the force of love;
Once more resumes the still successful lay,
Delighted thro' the verdant meads to stray.
O! come, invok'd, and pleas'd, with her repair
To breathe the balmy sweets of purer air;
In the cool evening negligently laid,
Or near the stream, or in the rural shade,
Propitious hear, and as thou hear'st, approve
The Gentle Shepherd's tender tale of love.

He is a gentle shepherd because, though apparently only a humble shepherd, his gentle birth is discovered at the end as is the equally gentle birth of the apparently lowly rustic girl he is in love with. This of course is an old folk theme. And the various ways of handling rustic dialect in the play reflect a debate on the language of pastoral that had been going on in England for some time. But the situation in Scotland was special. Though the arguments about the nature and proper language of pastoral put forward by Pope, Gay, Ambrose Philips and others south of the Border have some bearing on Ramsay's practice in *The Gentle Shepherd*, the fact that Scots was a distinguishing national speech and not simply a rustic dialect complicates the issue. There is some very effective vernacular Scots in Ramsay's play, both in the dialogue and in the interspersed songs (which are set to folk tunes). It is interlaced with standard English in varying degrees. Sometimes the true accent of vernacular speech can be heard:

Last morning I was gay and early out,
Upon a dyke I lean'd, glowring about,
I saw my Meg come linkan o'er the lee;
I saw my Meg, but Peggy saw na me;

For yet the sun was wading thro' the mist,
And she was close upon me e'er she wist;
Her coats were kiltit, and did sweetly shaw
Her straight bare legs that whiter were than snaw.
Her cockernony snooded up fou sleek,
Her haffet locks hang waving on her cheek;
Her cheeks sae ruddy, and her een sae clear;
And O! her mouth's like ony hinny pear.
Neat, neat she was, in bustine waistcoat clean,
As she came skiffing o'er the dewy green:
Blythsome I cry'd, 'My bonny Meg, come here,
I ferly wherefore, ye're so soon asteer?
But I can guess, ye're gawn to gather dew.'
She scour'd away, and said, 'What's that to you?'
'Then, fare ye well, Meg-dorts, and e'en's ye like,'
I careless cry'd, and lap in o'er the dyke.
I trow, when that she saw, within a crack,
She came with a right thieveless errand back:
Miscaw'd me first; then bad me hound my dog,
To wear up three waff ewes stray'd on the bog.
I leugh; and saw did she; then with great haste
I clasp'd my arms about her neck and waist; . . .

This is a modified Scots, with the accent of conversation
moving in and out, alternating with more formal descriptive
lines. More unambiguously rustic characters, like the old
shepherd Glaud, speak a more consistent Scots:

Then wad he gar his butler bring bedeen
The nappy bottle ben, and glasses clean,
Whilk in our breast rais'd sic a blythsome flame
As gart us mony a time gae dancing hame . . .

Yet this is not a deliberately 'low' language. 'Blythsome flame'
is a literary phrase, and though 'blythsome' is used in older
Scottish poetry (as in 'The Blythsome Bridal') and 'blithe' is
a common word in Scots song, the Scots word for flame

would be 'low', still in common use throughout the eighteenth century. But 'gar', 'bedeen', 'nappy', 'ben', 'whilk', 'sic' and 'gart' are all Scots words—not Scots spellings or Scots pronunciations of English words. On the other hand, when Sir William Worthy, the exiled royalist laird who returns after the Restoration, comes on the scene, he speaks at times a slightly Scots-besprinkled English but at moments of climax and discovery he speaks standard English, and very formal English at that:

> Whose daughter's she that wears the Aurora gown,
> With face so fair, and locks a lovely brown?—
> How sparking are her eyes!—What's this I find!
> This girl brings all my sister to my mind:
> Such were the features once adorned a face,
> Which death too soon depriv'd of sweetest grace.

And Patie, the shepherd, discovered in the end to have been gentle after all, duly adopts a gentle—or genteel—speech:

> 'Tis now a crime to doubt: my joys are full,
> With due obedience to my parent's will.—
> Sir, with paternal love survey her charms,
> And blame me not for rushing to her arms: . . .

This was the language with which Ramsay himself started as a poet, a language he tried to perfect by practice at the Easy Club and by regular reading of English poets and essayists. In 1721 he wrote a patriotic poem called 'Tartana; or, The Plaid', using a language that owed nothing at all to a Scottish tradition either courtly or popular:

> Ye Caledonian beauties! who have long
> Been both the muse and subject of my song,
> Assist your bard, who in harmonious lays,
> Designs the glory of your plaid to raise.
> How my fond breast with blazing ardor glows,
> Whene'er my song on you just praise bestows!

Or take another couplet from this poem:

How decent is the plaid, when in the pew
It hides th' enchanting fair from ogler's view!

This style has not the poise of Pope or the confidence of Prior; there are hints of vulgarity underneath it. It reveals an attempt to find an expression that would find favour with the English arbiters of taste of the time, even when it expresses Scottish sentiments. In English poetry we can trace changes in diction and movement from the beginning of the so-called 'refinement of our numbers' through Dryden and Pope and writers of *vers de société* such as Prior and Gay. We can also trace the development of eighteenth-century mock-heroics and Milton-ising. Scottish poetry did not mutate from the courtly to the refined or from aristocratic kinds of wit to middle-class kinds of elegance or from the heroic to the mock-heroic in a develop-ment that one might call organic, or at least that one might safely correlate with the changing pattern of the social and cultural scene. The derivative refinement, the *willed* elegance, combined with a somewhat prim morality, found in the tone and language of so much eighteenth-century Scottish writing, both verse and prose, is what I call gentility. I would remind you again of Ramsay's version of 'Auld Lang Syne' which ends with the couple getting decently married.

Yet we must not forget the other Ramsay—not only the Ramsay who printed poems from the Bannatyne Manuscript in his collection *The Evergreen* and thus made available some of the poetry of the older Scottish makars for the first time in generations, and not only the Ramsay who himself wrote poems imitative of the older Scots style and language, but the Ramsay who could celebrate the low life of Edinburgh in vigorous urban Scots. Beside his discreet praise of the decency of the plaid we may set these stanzas lamenting the dead Maggy Johnstoun, who kept a pub just south of Edinburgh:

When we were weary'd at the gowff,
Then Maggy Johnston's was our howff;
Now a' our gamesters may sit dowff,
   Wi' hearts like lead,
Death wi' his rung rax'd her a yowff,
   And sae she died . . .

She brawly did a pease-scon toast
Biz i' the queff and flie the frost;
There we gat fou wi' little cost,
   And muckle speed,
Now wae worth death, our sport's a' lost,
   Since Maggy's dead.

This is a far cry from the courtly Scots of Alexander Scott and it is equally far from the genteel English that Ramsay employed when he tried to compensate for the lack of a Scots courtly style by borrowing what he considered English elegance. One might ask the question why Scotland after the Union of 1707 found herself unable to develop a distinctive 'high' literary style and had to adapt one from her southern neighbour. The answer is partly that the disintegration of Scots as a literary language for reasons I discussed in my first lecture had by now gone too far, so that Scots was regarded as for the most part suitable only for poems of rustic celebration or urban low life. Another part of the answer lies in the cultural uncertainty, what might indeed be called a crisis of national identity, that followed the Union of 1707. Yet another part of the answer must have something to do with the fact that more and more Scots wrote in standard English but spoke and (as Edwin Muir argued in a famous passage)[5] felt in Scots, so that their use of English can in a sense be compared with the use of Latin by Renaissance Humanists. (It is, incidentally, interesting that early eighteenth-century printers and editors like Thomas Ruddiman and Robert Freebairn tried to revive a Scoto-Latin culture, but it was too late in the day for that.) For the Humanists, Cicero wrote the only truly

54

elegant Latin, as indeed for generations of schoolboys after-wards, as in my own schooldays in Edinburgh, when our Latin prose compositions always had to be Ciceronian in style. Eighteenth-century Scottish writers, using a medium that was not their spoken language, inevitably made it as Ciceronian as they could. Of course, the language of Pope was not exactly the language of his daily speech either, but it was related to that language in a way that the English used by Scots in their writing was not related to the language of their daily speech. It is quite possible, perhaps indeed desirable, to write a formal prose—philosophical, descriptive, historical or scientific—in a wholly formal language that is removed from the language of daily speech, which is why eighteenth-century Scottish philosophers, historians and essayists often wrote with such admirable clarity and elegance, but poetry, where reason and emotion must go together, requires a language in which the whole man can speak. W. B. Yeats recorded how, looking back on his earliest poetry, he realised that it had been insufficiently nourished by the whole man and concluded that 'we should ascend out of common interests, the thoughts of the newspapers, or the market-place, of men of science, but only so far as we can carry the normal, passionate reasoning self, the personality as a whole.'[6] The problem of expressing the personality as a whole in Scottish poetry was endemic in the eighteenth century. Those who solved it—Robert Fergus-son up to a point, and Robert Burns—did so by balancing Scots and English in a way that combined spontaneity and formality. This was not an easy feat, and even Burns was far from successful in achieving it consistently. Those who simply turned to a formal English style, though they might succeed brilliantly in expository prose, rarely did so in poetry. And even prose could succumb to the curse of gentility.

An uneasy awareness that a neo-classic English poetic style was not wholly appropriate to a Scottish poet—at least not to one writing in Scotland—and that to write in it would risk generating a kind of artificiality that can be more ridiculous

than impressive seems to be behind Robert Fergusson's fondness for the English burlesque, mock-heroic style (popular-
ised by, for example, *The Splendid Shilling* of John Philips)
which parodies what it imitates. Though Fergusson could
write tinkling English pastoral verse as well as the next man
and imitations of Shenstone's elegies better than most when
he chose to write in English, his most characteristic English
poems are in the burlesque style. Here, for example, are some
lines from his poem 'Good Eating' recommending his
readers to take a walk to Duddingston and sample the fare
at the inn there (which still stands) or to go to Leith and
enjoy themselves at Lawson's tavern:

Ye who for health, for exercise, for air,
Oft saunter from *Edina*'s smoke-capt spires,
And, by the grassy hill or dimpl'd brook
An appetite revive, should oft-times stray
O'er *Arthur's seat's* green pastures to the town,
For *sheep-heads* and bone-bridges fam'd of yore,
That in our country's annals stands yclept,
Fair *Duddingstonia,* where you may be blest
With simple fare and vegetative sweets,
Freed from the clamours of the busy world.

Or, if for recreation you should stray
To *Leithian* shore, and breathe the keener air
Wafted from Neptune's empire of the main;
If appetite invite, and cash prevail,
Fly not your joints upon the homeward track,
Till L A W S O N, chiefest of the Scottish hosts!
To nimble-footed waiters give command
The cloth to lay.—Instinctively they come,
And lo! the table, wrapt in cloudy steams,
Groans with the weight of the transporting fare
That breathes frankincense on the guests around.

Fergusson, who had a better formal education than either

Ramsay or Burns, having attended both Dundee Grammar
School and St Andrews University, did not possess the
deference to established literary tastes and fashions that both
Ramsay and Burns exhibited on occasion. Burns adored
Henry Mackenzie's sentimental novel, *The Man of Feeling*,
esteeming it 'next to the Bible'. Fergusson mocked it with a
poem about a sentimental pig called 'The Sow of Feeling'.
Most Scottish writers reacted with reverence when Boswell
brought Dr Johnson to Scotland in 1773. Fergusson wrote
two ironic poems about Johnson. One was in Scots, entitled
'To the Principal and Professors of the University of St
Andrews, on their superb treat to Dr Samuel Johnson' and
ironically recommends to the lexicographer a diet of native
Scots dishes, including haggis and sheep's heid.

> ST ANDREWS town may look right gawsy,
> Nae GRASS will grow upon her cawsey,
> Nor wa'-flow'rs of a yellow dye,
> Glour dowy o'er her RUINS high,
> Sin SAMY's head well pang'd wi' lear
> Has seen the ALMA MATER there: . . .

In his poem 'To Dr Samuel Johnson: Food for a new
Edition of his Dictionary' Fergusson made cheerful fun out
of Johnson's Latinized style, implicitly mocking the Latiniza-
tion that was characteristic of much learned Scottish prose
(i.e. English written by Scotsmen) of the time:

> GREAT PEDAGOGUE, whose literanian lore,
> with syllable and SYLLABLE conjoin'd
> To transmutate and varyfy, has learn'd
> The whole revolving scientific names
> That in the alphabetic columns lie,
> Far from the knowledge of mortalic shapes,
> As we, who never can peroculate
> The miracles by thee miraculiz'd,
> The Muse silential long, with mouth apart
> Would give vibration to stagnatic tongue,

And loud encomiate thy puissant name,
Eulogiated from the green decline
Of Thames's banks to Scoticanian shores,
Where Loch-lomondian liquids undulize.

This was Fergusson mocking pretentious literary language.
It is not, of course, a just criticism of Johnson's language, but
it was a criticism of any language so ostentatiously bookish
that it proclaimed the educational status of its author. And
eighteenth-century Scots were prone to using such a language.
Fergusson's own happiest poetic style was a Scots made up
partly of the Edinburgh Scots he grew up with, of the
Aberdeenshire Scots of his parents, of the Fifeshire Scots he
learned in his St Andrews days, and of an older literary Scots
he acquired from books. It was a Scots that could accommodate classical references as easily as the language of the older
Scots poets could, although differently. Unlike Ramsay,
whose Scots was either rustic or urban low-life or antiquarian,
Fergusson was able to use a Scots with a *gravitas* resulting from
his awareness of a Scoto-Latin tradition of the kind Thomas
Ruddiman had tried to revive. It was, incidentally, in the
columns of the magazine founded and edited by Thomas
Ruddiman's nephew that Fergusson's poems first appeared.
Even when Fergusson was describing Edinburgh low life,
which he frequently did, he shows this greater richness of
language. He shows, too, not only his ability to give new
vitality to the Habbie Simson tradition but also his ability to
pick up the octosyllabic couplet from English poets and use
it as a natural vehicle for his Scots. Here is a passage from his
poem on Edinburgh, 'Auld Reekie':

FRAE joyous Tavern, reeling drunk
Wi' fiery Phizz, and Ein half sunk,
Behad the Bruiser, Fae to a'
That in the reek o' Gardies fa':
Close by his side, a feckless Race
O' Macaronies shew their Face,

And think they're free frae Skaith or Harm,
While Pith befriends their Leaders Arm:
Yet fearfu' aften o' their Maught,
They quat the Glory of the Faught
To this same Warrior wha led
Thae Heroes to bright Honour's Bed;
And aft the hack o' Honour shines
In Bruiser's Face wi' broken Lines:
Of them sad tales he tells anon,
Whan Ramble and whan Fighting's done;
And, like Hectorian, ne'er impairs
The Brag and Glory o' his Sairs.

Fergusson, who died in the public Bedlam of Edinburgh at
the age of twenty-four when Robert Burns was fifteen years
old, was perhaps the only poet in eighteenth-century Scotland
who could do without the genteel tradition. He found a style
for the Scots language that was available to him, a style assured
and strong, artful without being courtly. Burns recognised
Fergusson's achievement as soon as he found a copy of his
poems. As he wrote to Dr John Moore in the famous auto-
biographical letter of August 1787, he was reading Samuel
Richardson and Smollett and had largely given up writing
poetry when 'meeting with Fergusson's Scotch Poems, I
strung anew my wildly-sounding, rustic lyre with emulating
vigour'. Burns paid other tributes to Fergusson, whom he
called 'my elder brother in misfortune, / By far my elder brother
in the Muse'. Yet Fergusson would never have talked of his
'rustic lyre' as Burns did. Burns's pose as an unlettered rustic
taught only by Nature, the 'Heaven-taught ploughman' hailed
by Henry Mackenzie, was deliberately assumed to enable him
to be accepted by the arbiters of taste in Edinburgh, the *literati*
as they liked to call themselves, as a species of natural man who
could confront the genteel tradition as a privileged outsider:
this is precisely the object of his preface to the Kilmarnock
edition.

But was he really outside the genteel tradition? Here is an extract from a letter that he wrote to his father from Irvine (where he was sent to learn flax-dressing) in December 1781, a month before his twenty-third birthday:

> I am quite transported at the thought that ere long, perhaps very soon, I shall bid an eternal adiew to all the pains, and uneasiness and disquietudes of this weary life; for I assure you I am heartily tired of it, and, if I do not very much deceive myself I could contendedly and gladly resign it.—
>
> > The Soul uneasy & confin'd from home
> > Rests & expatiates in a life to come.
> >
> > > Pope.
>
> It is for this reason that I am more pleased with the 15th, 16th & 17th verses of the 7th Chapter of Rev:[n] than any ten times as many verses in the whole Bible, & would not exchange the noble enthusiasm with which they inspire me, for all that this world has to offer—As for this world I despair of ever making a figure in it.—I am not formed for the bustle of the busy nor the flutter of the Gay. I shall never again be capable of it.

The calculated sententiousness of tone was probably to please his father. But his pompous introduction of a quotation from Pope's *Essay on Man* shows exhibitionism as well. And what are we to make of his remark that 'I am not formed for the bustle of the busy nor the flutter of the Gay', presented to his father as though it were an original thought? Chapter fifty-five of Mackenzie's novel *The Man of Feeling* gives us the last speech of the dying Harley, the man of feeling himself. He is talking to his friend, and says, among other things: 'This world, my dear Charles, was a scene in which I never much delighted. I was not formed for the bustle of the busy, nor the dissipation of the gay: . . .' Burns was clearly pretending to belong—or perhaps at the moment really feeling that he belonged—to the polite world of fashionable sentimental languor. It was a world he never thereafter wholly rejected.

Three months after the letter from which I have quoted Burns wrote to his former teacher, John Murdoch, the young man who had drilled him and his brother in elegant English speech and taught him to read English poetry and prose from Shakespeare to his own day. Here is how it opens:

> Dear Sir,
>
> As I have an opportunity of sending you a letter without putting you to that expence which any production of mine would but ill repay; I embrace it with pleasure to tell you that I have not forgotten, nor never will forget, the many obligations I lie under to your kindness and friendship. I do not doubt, Sir, but you will wish to know what has been the result of all the pains of an indulgent father, and a masterly teacher; and I wish I could gratify your curiosity with such a recital as you would be pleased with; but that is what I am afraid will not be the case. I have, indeed, kept pretty clear of vicious habits; and in this respect, I hope, my conduct will not disgrace the education I have gotten, but, as a man of the world, I am most miserably deficient . . .

He is using the language of worldly sophistication to deny his worldly sophistication, very much in the sentimental fashion of the day. Later on in the letter he tells Murdoch that his favourite reading is Shenstone's Elegies, 'Thomson, Man of feeling, a book I prize next to the Bible, Man of the World, Sterne, especially his Sentimental journey, Macpherson's Ossian &c. these are the glorious models after which I endeavour to form my conduct, and 'tis incongruous, 'tis absurd to suppose that the man whose mind glows with sentiments lighted up at their sacred flame—the man whose heart distends with benevolence to all the human race—he "who can soar above this little scene of things" [a phrase from Thomson's *Seasons*] can he descend to mind the paultry concerns about which the terrae-filial race fret, and fume, and vex themselves? . . .'

This was Burns's normal epistolary style. Not that it always expressed sentiments like these, but he expressed himself in his letters in a consciously, almost self-consciously, elegant neo-classic English. He spoke that way, too, when he attended the drawing rooms of the *literati* and when he was lionised in Edinburgh in the winter of 1786–7. It is said by one who heard both Burns and David Hume speak that Burns when he spoke in genteel company had less of a Scots accent than David Hume. Yet with his Ayrshire friends and at home on the farm he of course spoke an Ayrshire Scots. Only in one surviving letter do we find him writing as he spoke. It is written to William Nicol, the irascible school-master at the High School at Edinburgh:

Kind, honest-hearted Willie,

I'm sitten down here, after seven and forty miles ridin, e'en as forjeskit and forniaw'd as a forfoughten cock, to gie you some notion o' my landlopperlike stravaguin sin the sorrowfu' hour that I sheuk hands and parted wi' auld Reekie.—

My auld, ga'd Gleyde o' a meere has huchyall'd up hill and down brae, in Scotland and England, as teugh and birnie as a vera devil wi' me.—It's true, she's as poor's a Sang-maker and as hard's a kirk, and tipper-taipers when she taks the gate first like a Lady's gentlewoman in a minuwae, or a hen on a het girdle, but she's a hauld, poutherie Girran for a' that; and has a stomach like Willie Stalker's meere that wad hae digeested tumbler-wheels, for she'll whip me aff her five stimparts o' the best aits at a down-sittin and ne'er fash her thumb.—When ance her ringbanes and spavies, her crucks and cramps, are fairly soupl'd, she beets to, beets to, and ay the hindmost hour the tightest.—I could wager her price to a thretty pennies that, for twa or three wook ridin at fifty mile a day, the deil-stickit a five gallopers acqueesh Clyde and Whithorn could cast saut in her tail.—

I hae dander'd owre a' the kintra frae Dumbar to Selcraig, and hae forgather'd wi' monie a guid fallow, and monie a well-far'd hizzie. I met wi' twa dink quines in particlar, ane o' them a sonsie, fine fodgel lass, baith braw and bonie; the tither was a clean-shankit, straught, tight, well-far'd winch, as blythe's a lintwhite on a flowerie thorn, and as sweet and modest's a new blawn plumrose in a hazle shaw. They were baith bred to mainers by the beuk, and onie ane o' them has as muckle smeddum and rumble-gumption as the half o' some Presbyteries that you and I baith ken.—They play'd me sic a deevil o' a shavie that I daur say if my harigals were turn'd out, ye wad see two nocks i' the heart o' me like the mark of a kail-whittle in a castock.

I was gaun to write to a lang pystle, but Gude forgie me, I gat mysell saw noutouriously bitchify'd the day after kail-time that I can hardly stoiter but and ben . . .

I'll be in Dumfries the morn gif the beast be to the fore and the branks bide hale.

Gude be wi' you, Willie! Amen—
Robt. Burns.

This was the same man who, calling himself Sylvander, wrote to Mrs Angus M'Lehose as Clarinda in language like this:

You cannot imagine, Clarinda (I like the idea of Arcadian names in a commerce of this kind) how much store I have set by the hopes of your future friendship. I don't know if you have a just idea of my character, but I wish you to see me *as I am*. I am, as most people of my trade are, a strange will o' wisp being; the victim too frequently of much imprudence and many follies. My great constituent elements are Pride and Passion: the first I have endeavoured to humanise into integrity and honour; the last makes me a Devotee to the warmest degree of enthusiasm, in Love, Religion, or Friendship; either of them or all together as I happen to be inspired. . . .

In his Commonplace Book, which he began in April 1783 when he was just over twenty-four years old, Burns could use some self-consciously genteel language. Here is the beginning of the very first entry:

Observations, Hints, Songs, Scraps of Poetry &c. by Robt Burness; a man who had little art in making money, and still less in keeping it; but was, however, a man of some sense, a great deal of honesty, and unbounded goodwill to every creature rational or irrational. As he was but little indebted to scholastic education, and bred at a plough-tail, his performance must be strongly tinctured with his unpolished, rustic way of life; but as I believe, they are really his own, it may be some entertainment to a curious observer of human-nature to see how a plough-man thinks, and feels, under the pressure of Love, Ambition, Anxiety, Grief with the like cares and passions, which, however diversified by the Modes, and Manners of life, operate pretty much alike I believe, in all the Species.

This is a *posed* prose and it is clearly meant for the eyes of some future genteel reader. Decency, propriety, gentility were qualities admired by the young Burns, however wild his own behaviour could be. In his very first poem, or at least in the poem which he records in his Commonplace Book as his very first poem, 'Handsome Nell', he pays tributes to the girl's possession of these qualities:

She dresses ay sae clean and neat,
 Both decent and genteel;
And then there's something in her gate
 Gars only dress look weel.

This juvenile song is an interesting combination of the folk tradition and of something more consciously refined—as so many eighteenth-century Scottish songs were. It begins

O once I lov'd a bonny lass
Ay and I love her still

64

And whilst that virtue warms my breast
I'll love my handsome Nell.

The first line is in the purest folk idiom; the second is a simply personal statement made in his own voice (and the rhyming of 'still' with 'Nell' shows that he was thinking of an Ayrshire Scots pronunciation); the third—'And whilst that virtue warms my breast'—is consciously 'literary'.

What did Burns mean by 'genteel'? He uses it with reference to the way Nell dressed, and this fits in exactly with definition number four of the word in the Oxford English Dictionary: 'Of persons: Gentlemanly or ladylike in appearance; well-dressed.' This is illustrated from several eighteenth-century quotations, including one from Goldsmith's *She Stoops to Conquer*: 'Did I not work that waistcoat, to make you genteel?' Gentility is a *surface* thing; it is a matter of outward appearance and adornment. You could be genteel without being decent, for Burns specifically says that Nell's dress was both decent and genteel; that is, a gentlemanly or ladylike outward appearance had no necessary connection with real decency. But I do not wish to press this point or to take Burns's 'both . . . and' too literally. It is the outwardness of gentility, being a matter of style rather than substance, that I wish to stress.

Burns was drawn to the genteel tradition as established in eighteenth-century Scotland by the *literati*. His formal educa-tion, given by his tutor John Murdoch, was entirely in that tradition. The vernacular folk tradition as well as the older 'art' tradition of Scots poetry Burns discovered for himself. Trotted through the drawing-rooms of the *literati* in Edin-burgh and invited by country gentlemen to their estates, Burns was continually tempted to write entirely in the Scottish version of late neo-classic English, a genteel language rather than an organically developed literary language. He some-times did so; more often he grafted elements of that style on to a largely or partly Scots vocabulary; and often again he wrote in the pure folk style or in a cultivated Scots poetic style he inherited through Fergusson. It was an extraordinary balancing act, both in his life and in his art. Carried out of his rustic background into the worldly sophistication of the minor characters of the Scottish Enlightenment (he met none of the major figures, through an accident of chronology), he could have adopted as his regular idiom the kind of thing we find, for example, in *A Collection of Original Poems, by The Rev. Mr Blacklock, and other Scotch Gentlemen* published in Edinburgh in 1760. Here is the opening of a drinking song in this collection:

> With roses and with myrtles crown'd,
> I triumph; let the glass go round.
> Jovial Bacchus, ever gay,
> Come, and crown the happy day;
> From my breast drive every care;
> Banish sorrow and despair:
> Let social mirth, and decent joy,
> This delightful hour employ.

Burns, fortunately, turned to another tradition for his drinking songs:

> We are na fou, we're nae that fou,
>   But just a drappie in our e'e;
> The cock may craw, the day may daw,
>   And ay we'll taste the barley bree.
>
> It is the moon, I ken her horn,
>   That's blinkin in the lift sae hie;
> She shines sae bright to wyle us hame,
>   But by my sooth she'll wait a wee!
>
> We are na fou, &c.

Burns's drinking song is deliberately not *respectable*, any more than *The Jolly Beggars* (the name generally given to Burns's 'Cantata' *Love and Liberty*) is respectable. Gentility implies respectability; you could be poorly dressed but still genteel. In Henry Mackenzie's periodical *The Lounger* there is an essay (13 July 1779) describing the misfortunes of a poor orphan girl. The author encounters her in St Andrew's Square, and the first thing he notices is that she is 'meanly dressed'. He goes on:

> When I passed her, she turned a little towards me, and made a sort of halt; but said nothing. I am ill at looking any body full in the face; so I went on a few steps before I turned my eye to observe her. She had, by this time, resumed her former pace. I remarked a certain elegance in her form, which the poorness of her garb could not altogether over-come; her person was thin and genteel, and there was something not ungraceful in the stoop of her head, and the seeming feebleness with which she walked.

The girl is unfortunate, but determinedly respectable, and worthy of the author's charitable offices. Of course, there is a tradition of the warm-hearted prostitute prevalent at this time, and this cuts across the whole idea of gentility. This senti-mental tradition touched Burns too; he often professed that the good heart is all, and eclipses any other moral qualities. There is a complex relationship between sentimentality and gentility in Scotland which is worth some detailed investiga-tion, but here I can only mention it.

One of the features of Scottish gentility which distinguished it from the English variety is its relation to the whole question of national identity and the use of a differentiating Scots language. Because Scots had not its centre of cultural author-ity, because it was no longer an accepted living literary language reflecting back on and enriching the spoken lan-guage while at the same time being enriched by it, people did not know to place it. It was quaint and old; or it was common; or it was rustic; or it was, as David Hume held, 'a very corrupt dialect' of English. Gentility of speech was thus bound up with an escape from Scots. In 1787, at the very time when Burns was being lionised in Edinburgh as the 'Heaven-taught ploughman', the Aberdeen minor poet and philo-sopher James Beattie brought out his book entitled *Scotticisms, arranged in Alphabetical Order, designed to correct Improprieties of Speech and Writing*. His aim, he says in his introduction, is 'to put young writers and speakers on their guard against some of those Scotch idioms, which, in this country, are liable to be mistaken for English. With respect to broad Scotch words I do not think any caution requisite, as they are easily known, and the necessity of avoiding them is obvious.' He apologises for his strictness, but explains that 'where the purity of language is concerned, it is, in *my* opinion, more safe to be too scrupul-ous, than too little so.' He considers that English was 'brought to perfection in the days of Addison and Steele' and deplores 'every unauthorised word and idiom' that has been introduced since their time. His aim is thus Ciceronian; he regarded good English as the Humanists regarded good Latin as fixed at a particular period in its history and believes it to be the duty of a writer, even (or perhaps especially) a Scottish writer, to imitate the style of that period and avoid words and usages introduced subsequently.

Some of Beattie's Scotticisms are now accepted as standard English and some of his vulgarities of speech are no longer considered so. 'Come here,' he says, is wrong; it should be 'come hither.' Many lively and expressive Scots usages are condemned, many of which are genuine Scots descended from Middle Scots usage. He will not allow Scots to say baxter, brewster, dyster or webster, insisting on baker, brewer, dyer, weaver. But he allows maltster, spinster, punster, songster and tapster because they are normal in standard English. 'The Scots think it genteel to call a man *dull*, rather than *deaf*. But *dull* is *stupid. Dull of hearing* is proper.'

One characteristic of genteel writing is the reluctance to call a spade a spade. 'Tropes and figures,' says Beattie in his *Essays on Poetry and Music*, 'are favourable to delicacy. When the proper name of a thing is in any respect unpleasant, a well-chosen trope will convey the idea in such a way as to give no offence. This is agreeable, and even necessary, in polite conversation, and cannot be dispensed with in elegant writing of any kind.' A fondness for euphuism and sometimes pretentiousness is characteristic both of educated Scots speech and of American speech. One could go into the question of gentility in American speech in great detail: the substitution of 'casket' for 'coffin', 'mortician' for 'undertaker'; 'elevator' for 'lift', to say nothing of those monstrous coinages such as 'washeteria', 'laundromat' (on the curious assumption that the element 'mat' means 'self-operating', taking the 'mat' element in 'automatic' to mean what in fact is meant by the 'auto' element) and so on; the preference of 'automobile' for 'car', 'locomotive' for 'engine' and in general the longer word for the shorter is an aspect of American gentility that is the other side of the coin that gives us expressive American slang. But that is another subject. I would simply like to draw attention to common elements in American and Scottish gentility of speech.

What I have called the 'ciceronianism' of Scottish writers, part of the attempt to achieve a high cultured expression when there was no natural arbiter of such expression, has persisted in Scottish life for generations. E. M. W. Tillyard once remarked that the exchange of letters between the hero and his friend at the opening of Scott's *Redgauntlet* is couched in a language too artificial for it ever to have been used by young men writing to each other in eighteenth-century Scotland. He was wrong; that was exactly how young men in Scotland did write to each other and how they continued to write and even speak for a long time afterwards. Even in my own student days in Edinburgh I remember it as a common occurrence for members of the University's Diagnostic Society (the other societies were the Philomathic and the Dialectic) to rise after a member had spoken and say: 'I rise to homologate the sentiments of the previous speaker'. Only in Scotland could the word 'homologate' be common in student parlance.

The rise of gentility in Scotland is associated with the rise of Moderatism in religion. Moderatism in its earlier phase seems wholly attractive to the modern mind: it represented reason, common sense, humanity, in a word enlightenment, against the extreme claims of a narrow Calvinism. Most of us today, if and when we look back on the ecclesiastical history of eighteenth-century Scotland, would associate ourselves with New Licht against Auld Licht. But as the century wore on and the impetus of the Scottish Enlightenment became blunted, Moderatism became more and more reverence of established authority and insistence on respectability and gentility. The intolerance and zealotry of the Auld Lichts, so effectively satirised by Burns, came more and more to look like independence and national freedom. The great debate over church patronage—whether parish ministers should be appointed by their congregations or by representatives of the Establishment—was brought to a head in the great Disruption of 1843, when hundreds of ministers and elders walked out from the General Assembly to form the Free Church of Scotland. Lord Cockburn, who was an enlightened observer of the Scottish scene as well as an interesting writer with an unusual sensibility, observed what happened with astonished admiration. 'The fact of above 450 clerical members of an Establishment, being above a third of its total complement, casting it off, is sufficient to startle anyone who considers the general adhesiveness of churchmen to their sect and their endowments. But when this is done under no bodily persecu- tion, with no accession of power, from no political motive, but purely from dictates of conscience, the sincerity of which is attested by the sacrifice not merely of professional station and emoluments but of all worldly interests, it is one of the rarest occurrences in moral history. I know of no parallel to it. . . . They have abandoned that public station which was the ambition of their lives, and have descended from certainty to precariousness, and most of them from comfort to destitution, solely for their principles.'

Evangelicalism now became in a sense associated with democracy and Scottish national feeling (as it had done in some ways in the time of the Covenanters) and the Establishment went on comfortably with its lukewarm respectable religion, its conformity to authority, and its genteel culture. The situation did not remain like this. The rise of Kailyard literature brought a new kind of sentimentality into association with Wee Free religion. But the decline of Moderatism from its association with the Scottish Enlightenment into an uncreative respectability and gentility, which began in the late eighteenth century and continued in the nineteenth, was felt in many areas of Scottish national life. One finds it, for example, in the development in both Edinburgh and Glasgow of an affected genteel accent—known in Edinburgh as Morningside and in Glasgow as Kelvinside—employed in a conscious effort to display a removal from common Scots speech. The joke is, of course, that both these accents represent a purely Scottish phenomenon. I shall discuss this phenomenon in greater detail in my next lecture.

NOTES

1. James Kinsley, Ed., *Scottish Poetry; A Critical Survey,* London, 1955, p.14.
2. Quoted in Maurice Lindsay, *History of Scottish Literature,* London, 1977, p.35.
3. David Craig, *Scottish Literature and the Scottish People, 1680-1830,* London, 1961, p.20.
4. Kenneth Buthlay, 'Habbie Simson', in *Bards and Makars,* Glasgow, 1977.
5. Edwin Muir, *Scott and Scotland,* London, 1936, pp.29-30.
6. W. B. Yeats, *The Cutting of an Agate,* London, 1912, p.70.

III

THE REBELLION AGAINST GENTILITY

The search for gentility in eighteenth-century Scotland went on side by side with a great deal of drunkenness, bawdy conviviality and coarseness of speech. Looking back from the second decade of the nineteenth century Robert Chambers recorded what he called the 'conviviala of the preceding age' with fascinated horror. 'Tavern dissipation, now so rare among the respectable classes of the community, formerly prevailed in Edinburgh to an incredible extent', he wrote in his *Traditions of Edinburgh*, 'and engrossed the leisure hours of all professional men, scarcely excepting even the most stern and dignified.' In innumerable clubs and societies, ranging from the most elegant gatherings of the *literati* to the most riotous of tavern meetings, eighteenth-century Edinburgh citizens imbibed a variety of alcoholic drinks from the gentlemanly claret to humble tippenny; gin or whisky with oysters or rizzard haddocks was consumed in Edinburgh's many oyster taverns (for at that time the Firth of Forth still teemed with oysters). Robert Fergusson celebrated varieties of Edinburgh roystering. Robert Burns when in Edinburgh attended drinking and singing sessions at the Crochallan Fencibles, for whom he produced his collection of bawdy songs known as *The Merry Muses of Caledonia*. It is of course perfectly reasonable to expect those outside the circle of gentility to engage in such activities; what is interesting about eighteenth-century Scotland is the degree to which gentility and coarseness co-existed in the same circles. This was to some extent true in eighteenth-century England as well as in Scotland, but the dichotomy was more marked in Scotland. If we look for example at the life of Lord Kames, the distinguished law/ lord, essayist, literary critic, philosopher and agricultural improver, we find in his writings a tone of elegant rumination quite at odds with what Ramsay of Ochtertyre called his 'levity or prurience of speech'. Kames's favourite term, both of affection and reproach, applied to members of either sex, was 'bitch', and he once said of himself that 'I ken very weel that I am the coarsest and most black/avised bitch in a' the Court o' Session'. On his last visit to the Court, shortly before his death in his eighty/seventh year, he took farewell of his legal brethren with the exclamation, 'Fare ye a' weel, ye bitches!' Kames was not as hard a drinker as a younger colleague on the bench, Lord Newton. 'He considered himself,' says Chambers, 'as only the better fitted for business, that he had previously imbibed six bottles of claret; and one of his clerks afterwards declared that the best paper he ever knew his lord/ ship dictate, was done after a debauch where that amount of liquor had fallen to his share.' There are numerous well/ attested stories of dinner parties where the guests were carried away drunk to bed by servants specially employed for that purpose; some of these guests were judges who appeared on the Bench the following morning.

Some judges, like James Boswell's father Lord Auchinleck, despised any attempt to imitate the manners and speech of Englishmen and cultivated an aggressive Scots on the bench. So did Lord Braxfield, the original of R. L. Stevenson's *Weir of Hermiston,* who was notorious for what Ramsay of Och/ tertyre calls 'the liveliness, the coarseness, the harshness, of his . . . expression in trials of life and death.' But in Braxfield's case his cultivated coarseness was part of his general refusal to come to terms with the genteel Establishment of the *literati.* 'With the *tonish* philosophers and *literati* of Edinburgh,' wrote Ramsay, 'he had little connection or correspondence. Certain it is, he disliked their principles, and was aware of their con/ sequences. Nor was he a metaphysician or *belles lettres* scholar.' In holding out for an older, Scottish tradition, he had inevitably to support a tradition of vernacular coarseness, for no purely native tradition of elegance survived the end of Scottish courtliness. Sometimes an assured Scots could be employed in descriptions of urban conviviality, as in so many of Fergusson's poems; but Fergusson was a special case. When Burns wanted to celebrate Edinburgh in a duty poem of thanks for the hospitality he had received from the *literati,* he adopted a tone of pretentious gentility that comes through unmistakeably in the unfortunate opening lines:

Edina! Scotia's darling seat!
All hail thy palaces and tow'rs,
Where once beneath a Monarch's feet,
Sat Legislation's sov'reign pow'rs!

This is a far cry from what he sang at meetings of the Croch-allan Fencibles and just as far, though in a different direction, from his irreverent parodying of the classicising gentility which had been invading Scottish song since the time of Allan Ramsay:

When maukin bucks, at early f- -s,
In dewy glens are seen, Sir;
And birds, on boughs, take of their m- -s,
Amang the leaves sae green, Sir;
Latona's sun looks liquorish on
Dame Nature's grand impetus,
Till his p- -go rise, then westward flies
To r- -ger Madame Thetis.

This is the first stanza of a song Burns called 'Ode to Spring' and set to a traditional tune called 'The tither morn'.

So there were rebellions against the genteel tradition even among those who sometimes succumbed to it and kinds of ungenteel speech and behaviour even by those whose writings showed a carefully cultivated gentility. A determined use of the Scots vernacular in speech, even if it was not carried into writing, can be seen as an assertion of Scottish nationhood and there can be little doubt that it was sometimes intended as such. As the nineteenth century developed, the use of Scots by educated and respectable people steadily decreased, so that Henry Mackenzie (who was born in 1745 and lived until 1831), looking back in old age, could recall: 'There was a pure classical *Scots* spoken by genteel people, which I thought very agreeable; it had nothing of the coarseness of the vulgar *patois* of the lower orders of the people.' Scots continued in the nineteenth century as the vehicle for pallid imitations of Burns and for comic songs and recitations of the kind collected in the egregious anthology of verse entitled *Whistlebinkie,* one of the most popular collections of the century.

The paradox of coarseness of manners and elegance of writing did not survive the eighteenth century. Mackenzie records the decline of swearing and gives examples of eighteenth-century outbursts. 'Sir Robert Myreton of Gogar' he wrote, 'was the most inveterate swearer in Scotland. He could not speak a sentence without an oath.' He tells us that the celebrated Italian singer Tenducci, who made such a hit in Edinburgh in the early 1770s, retained a vivid recollection of Sir Robert (who was fond of music) but, not recalling his name, described him as 'il cavaliere che sempre dice, *Goddam*'. Mackenzie continues:

> Sir Robert always said grace at his own table. One day a clergyman dined with him, and forgetting the etiquette of asking the reverend gentleman to say grace, Sir Robert began to say it himself; he suddenly recollected the impropriety, but was too far on to stop, and finished his grace in the following extraordinary manner: 'O Lord! ... God's curse! .... Deil care! .... Amen!'

Gentility of the written word moved into a more general area of social gentility and determined respectability as the nineteenth century progressed. Examples of this are abundant. A minor one, which I have always found amusing, is again recorded by Mackenzie: 'Thigging a good custom: a new married couple going round their friends and relations for assistance to set up house; has softened into wedding presents.'

What one might call the new respectability, which went with a decline in the use of the vernacular, in swearing, in heavy drinking and in bawdry, did not necessarily mean an increase in real delicacy of either speech or behaviour. Once more I cite an appealing bit of evidence by Mackenzie, who recorded the loss of a kind of delicacy prevalent in his young days in the eighteenth century: 'There was one delicate piece of politeness, which I never saw carried so far as in Edinburgh in my younger days, that of never producing children before any lady who had no family or who had lost her children. I well remember being forbid to come to tea when any friend of my mother's in either of those predicaments came to visit her.'

I have mentioned the co-existence in eighteenth-century Scotland of gentility of the written word, and coarseness of speech and behaviour. This Jekyll-and-Hyde syndrome may be connected with that yoking together of opposites to which Gregory Smith gave the deliberately comic-pretentious term 'the Caledonian antisyzygy' a term gleefully pounced on by the modern Scottish poet Hugh MacDiarmid as descriptive of a characteristic Scottish paradox. But if 'antisyzygy' is a Scottish characteristic, it is perhaps connected with pulls in different directions that Scottish culture suffered from at least since 1603. (Though to be fair to the antisyzygy mongers, they see it as equally characteristic of mediaeval Scottish poetry.) The most striking example in real life of the Jekyll-and-Hyde syndrome can be seen in the career of Deacon Brodie, respectable Edinburgh citizen, Deacon of Wrights, member of the Town Council, talented cabinet-maker, by day, and by night a daring burglar. He went too far when he and an accomplice decided to rob the General Excise Office for Scotland on the night of 5 March 1788. Betrayed by his accomplice, he fled the country but was eventually arrested in

Amsterdam and brought back to Scotland where, after a dramatic trial presided over by Lord Braxfield, he was found guilty and condemned to death. On 1 October 1788 he was hanged on a gibbet that he had himself designed for the Edin-burgh civic authorities. In an upstairs room of the house at 17 Heriot Row, Edinburgh, where Robert Louis Stevenson grew up, there was a bureau made by Brodie. Stevenson was fascinated by Brodie's story and for years worked with W.E.Henley on a play on his life. The theme of the co-existence of opposites never ceased to haunt Stevenson; it received its most explicit treatment in 1885 in *Strange Case of Dr Jekyll and Mr Hyde*. Underneath Victorian respectability something very different lay in wait.

Stevenson himself provides one of the clearest examples of the rebellion against gentility in nineteenth-century Scotland. By this time we are in the sixth and seventh decade of the nineteenth century, in the heart of the Victorian era. The recrudescence of evangelical religion symbolised and in a sense heralded by the Disruption of 1843 and the accompany-ing decline of Moderatism as a cultural force, the softening of manners, the encroachment of gentility into all phases of life in addition to literature, the entrenchment of Victorian respectability, made for a much more black-and-white picture than that which meets us in the eighteenth century. In eighteenth-century Edinburgh, drunkenness and coarseness of speech and sometimes sexual licence too could co-exist with high social pretentions and cultivated elegance of writing. By the mid-nineteenth century the two worlds had moved completely apart. The strong-minded ladies of the eighteenth century, so often remarked on by visitors for their outspokenness and independence of mind, could read novels such as *Tom Jones* which were not regarded as suitable reading for ladies of the nineteenth century. Ministers congratulated themselves on what they considered this improvement in manners and morals. This particular development could of course be paralleled in England, but within Scotland the

dichotomy took on a special character. The willed Bohemianism that Stevenson indulged in with his cousin Bob Stevenson
and his friend Charles Baxter was intended as a defiance of
that special Scottish kind of gentility that was associated with
Scottish religion and, paradoxically, also with a defensiveness
about Scottish language and Scottish identity. They practised
what they called 'Jink' and defined as 'doing the most absurd
acts for the sake of their absurdity': this was a slap in the face
equally of Calvinism, with its deeply serious view of all
action and motivation, and of the Calvinist-derived doctrine
of hard work and success. We do not have to accept completely the Weber-Tawney thesis about the association of
Calvinism with a capitalist individualist view of material
success as proof of divine blessing to realise that some such
view became established in Scottish middle-class society as
Moderatism declined and evangelical modes of Christianity
moved into the central ground of bourgeois attitudes and
behaviour. Stevenson's quarrel with his father, whom he
loved but whose basic views he could not bring himself to
accept, was partly a quarrel about Christian theology and
partly a quarrel about the way to evaluate human behaviour.
Stevenson equated respectability with hypocrisy and, by
extension, for a period at least he equated vice with honesty.
When he haunted the 'howffs' of Lothian Road and Leith
Walk, associating with prostitutes and social outcasts, he was
deliberately thumbing his nose at Edinburgh gentility:

O fine, religious, decent folk,
  In Virtue's flaunting gold and scarlet,
I sneer between two puffs of smoke—
  Give me the publican and harlot.

His private poems as a young man show him boasting of
this attitude:

I walk the streets smoking my pipe
And I love the dallying shop-girl
That leans with rounded stern to look at the fashions;

78

And I hate the bustling citizen,
The eager and hurrying man of affairs I hate,
Because he bears his intolerance writ on his face
And every movement and word of him tells me how much
                                        he hates me.

I love night in the city,
The lighted streets and the swinging gait of harlots.
I love cool pale morning,
In the empty bye-streets,
With only here and there a female figure,
A slavey with lifted dress and a key in her hand,
A girl or two at play in a corner of waste-land
Tumbling and showing their legs and crying out
                                        to me loosely.

This was a very different Edinburgh from the one Stevenson
inhabited with his parents in Heriot Row, where his mother
would show him off, at tea parties to her friends in the
drawing-room, dressed in his velvet jacket, to be acclaimed
as a 'young Heine with a Scottish accent'. *This* kind of
Bohemianism was acceptable to the genteel: a taste for
literature and velvet jackets—even for amateur theatricals—
was not necessarily a sign of the devil's having taken over, and
it is interesting that long after Stevenson's death respectable
Edinburgh citizens recalled with nostalgia what they considered his harmless and engaging Bohemian ways. They
knew nothing of his consorting with prostitutes, nothing of
the Edinburgh night life which, in sharp distinction to that
of the eighteenth century, went on in places and at times
unknown to the ordinary respectable citizen. They knew
nothing, either, of the curious games he played with his life-
long friend Charles Baxter. Baxter was a respectable Edinburgh solicitor, a Writer to the Signet, but there was a side
to him, apparently revealed only to Stevenson, that relished
practical jokes, irreverence and genteel nose-thumbing at the
genteel world.

Sometimes Baxter and Stevenson would take these gestures to remarkable lengths. Long after he had left Edinburgh Stevenson managed to enlist Baxter's aid in epistolary jokes at the expense of the respectable. In June 1886, an established writer recently made famous by the publication of *Dr Jekyll and Mr Hyde*, Stevenson, then living in Bournemouth, answered a London house agent's advertisement with the following letter:

> Dear Sirs,
>
> Observing in today's *Daily News* the advertisement of a house at Nunhead, and being myself on the move, I write to ask you to communicate with my lawyer, Mr Charles Baxter, Writer to the Signet, 11 S. Charlotte Street, Edinburgh, and oblige
>
> Yours truly,
Byron McGuiness

The house agents duly wrote to Baxter with details of the house offered for sale, and Baxter, who caught on at once to what Stevenson was doing, replied:

> Dear Sirs,
>
> Please pay no attention to anything that comes from that man McGuinness. He is simply a monomaniac who knowing I have recently succeeded to some money pesters my life with what he considers eligible investments. I don't as it happens usually live in houses at £30.
>
> May I ask if McG. has mooted any question of commission?
>
> Yours truly,

Completely fooled, the house agents sent the McGuinness letter to Baxter, and Baxter replied:

> Dear Sirs,
>
> I return Mr Byron McGuinness's letter. I did not know that it was in the capacity of his adviser that you had been

requested to write to me.

Some years ago, I did some business for him, but my bill has never been paid. What I would willingly submit to if I could only never hear his accursed name again!

Yours truly,

This is only one of many such games that Stevenson and Baxter played together at the expense of innocent business men. Another one involved a man called A. Douglas Noll who had advertised for people with money to invest to become directors in his new company formed to manufacture cheap portable sewing machines. Stevenson answered the advertisement, writing as Byron McGuinness and explained that Charles Baxter was his agent. Noll then wrote to Baxter and Baxter replied (under his own name, as he always did) explaining that 'Mr McGuinness is a very shrewd man, and any arrangements as to my look-out must be strictly confidential'. The man they played with most cruelly was one George Thomson of Kent who advertised for people willing to invest £1,000 in his electric paint remover. They baited him mercilessly, and when Baxter suggested that his business was below the dignity of his client, Thomson replied angrily citing the distinguished fellow members of the club to which he belonged. This gave Baxter (who was more active in the affair than Stevenson) the chance to polish Thomson off with a freezing reply: 'If you are a man of business you ought to know that a parade of high sounding names such as you mention has no effect except to make one smile at the Cockney simplicity that imagines anyone will be influenced by them; but apparently the senile Tory belief in the virtue of the aristocracy is not yet extinct.'

Though the victims in these cases were Englishmen, the game itself was an extension of a revolt against Edinburgh respectability that developed in Stevenson's student days. With Baxter, Bob Stevenson and other friends, Stevenson founded a society whose constitution began with the words:

'Disregard everything our parents taught us.' (It was Stevenson's father's discovery of this document that initiated the great crisis between them.) He was still dodging what he called 'the thunderbolt of parental anger' when he wrote to Baxter from France in July 1877 recalling their Bohemian times together in Edinburgh: 'the past where we have been drunk and sober, and sat outside of grocers' shops on fine dark nights, and wrangled in the Speculative [the debating society to which they belonged], and heard mysterious whistling in Waterloo Place, and met missionaries from Aberdeen; generally, the past.'

The most entertaining and the most obviously Scottish of the games Stevenson and Baxter played together involved nobody but themselves. Under the assumed names of Johnson or Johnstone (Baxter) and Thomson (Stevenson), two Scots-speaking religious hypocrites, they exchanged letters in broad Scots. This kind of role-taking came naturally to both of them, and with Stevenson it was associated with the whole Jekyll-and-Hyde syndrome I have already discussed. Here is Thomson writing to Johnson from France in May 1884:

My first name is Dauvit. Do ye mind when I was a baker at Kirkintilloch? Yon were braw days! And when I keepit a wee, bit, tosh, laigh, canny dram shop at Camlang? Eh, it was grand! Noo, I'm a mere wauf, randy beggarman . . .

The masterpiece is a letter from Stevenson (this time as Johnstone) to Baxter (as Thomson) explaining how he had been caught stealing from the church collection-plate and so had left the Church of Scotland to join the sect of Morrisonians:

It's done. I'm a dissenter. I kenned fine frae the beginning hoo it would a' end; I saw there was nae justice for auld Johnstone. The last I tauld ye, they had begun a clash aboot the drink. O sic a disgrace! when, if no onything, I rayther drink less nor mair since yon damned scandal aboot

82

the blue ribbon. I took the scunner as faur back as that, Thomson; and O man, I wuss that I had just left the estayblishment that very day! But no, I was aye loyal like them that went afore me.

Weel, the ither day, up comes yon red-heedit, pishion-faced creeter—him a minister! 'Mr Johnstone,' says he, 'I think it my duty to tell 'ee that there's a most unpleisand fama aboot you.' 'Sir,' says I, 'they take a pleasure to per-secute me. What is't noo?'

What was't? Man, Thomson, I think shame to write it: *No Bony-Feed wi' the plate.* Is'n that peetiful? The auld, auld story! The same weary, auld havering claver 'at they tauld aboot Sandie Sporran—him that was subsekently hanged, ye'll mind. And wi' me—hoo improabable! But it a' comes o' that silly hash aboot my brither Sandy's trust: a thankless office, the trustees!

Whatever, I saw that I was by wi't. Says I, 'I leave the Kirk.' 'Weel,' says he, 'I think you're parfitly richt' and a wheen mair maist unjudeecial and unjudeecious observa-tions. Noo, I'm a Morrisonian, an I like it fine. We're a sma' body, but unco tosh. The prezentar's auld, tae; an' if ye'll meet in wi' our opeenions—some o' them damned hetrodox by my way o't, but a body cannae have a'thing—I mak nae mainner o' doobt but what ye micht succeed him. I'm a great light in the body; much sympathy was felt for me generally among the mair leeberal o' a' persuasions: a man at my time o' life and kent sae lang!

This from the pen of a man who as a small boy liked to play at being a minister preaching and praying and whose earliest written work of any significance was a history of a rising by the Covenanters written from their point of view. Stevenson is here satirising not only hypocrisy but the whole tenor of small-town religion, with its ministers and elders and regular church-goers, its gossiping and back-biting and above all the disparity between religious language and actual behaviour. This is the very stuff of what later came to be called the fiction of the Kailyard, represented by J. M. Barrie's *Auld Licht Idylls, A Window in Thrums* and *The Little Minister,* S. R. Crockett's *The Stickit Minister* and *The Lilac Sunbonnet,* and Ian Maclaren's (pen-name of Dr John Watson, like Crockett a Free Church Minister) collection of stories and sketches entitled *Beside the Bonnie Brier Bush* and *The Days of Auld Langsyne.* Kailyard fiction, long despised as a sentimental rendering of Scottish small-town life that evades the realities in favour of contrived and sickly inventions, has recently come in for some interesting re-valuation. It has been pointed out by Eric Anderson, for example, that Barrie's Thrums is 'far from idyllic' and the dominie who tells the stories in *A Window in Thrums* 'hints ever and again at the sadness which lies ahead'.[1] Yet one cannot deny the coy sentimentality so often found in the work of Crockett and Ian Maclaren, even though their rendering of local Scots in dialogue is often accurate, convincing and lively.

The Kailyard writers wrote in the last dozen years of the nineteenth century. The kind of denigrating critical humour shown in the Johnson-Thomson letters of Stevenson and Baxter does not recur anywhere else during the remainder of the century, when literature with a genuinely Scottish flavour narrowed down more and more to stories of small-town life that were, in Eric Anderson's words, 'both churchy and sentimental'. The title 'Kailyard' comes from a song (to be found in James Johnson's *Scots Musical Museum* to which Burns contributed so much), two lines of which were printed as an epigraph to *Beside the Bonnie Brier Bush*:

> There grows a bonnie brier bush in our kail-yard,
> And white are the blossoms on't in our kail-yard.

The attack on the Kailyard was first mounted by the man who chose the name for this kind of literature, the Edinburgh advocate and literary historian J. H. Millar, whose article entitled 'The Literature of the Kailyard' appeared in W.E. Henley's *New Review* for May–June 1895. Millar followed up this attack with a sharp denunciation of the movement in his *Literary History of Scotland* (1903) in which he described how, as a result of the writing of Barrie and others, 'the land was plangent with the sobs of grown men, vainly endeavour- ing to stifle emotion by an elaborate affectation of "peching" and "hoasting".'

There is a relationship between gentility and sentimentality, and it can be traced in Scottish life and letters at least from the time of Henry Mackenzie's novel *The Man of Feeling* (1771). The discipline of feeling by traditions of craftsmanship that require the objectifying of emotion into formal channels largely disappeared in Scottish literature with the departure of the Court and the resulting decline of the courtly tradition in poetry and music. We have seen how Robert Fergusson, virtually alone among Scots poets of the eighteenth century, was able to avoid sentimentality by the sureness of his verbal craftsmanship in Scots. Burns was an equally good craftsman —at his best a better one—but he never had any certainty of taste and he could follow up the finely articulated 'To a Mouse', with its restrained handling of personal emotion, with the artificially sentimental 'To a Mountain Daisy', just as he could interpolate into 'The Cotter's Saturday Night' stanzas (such as the opening one addressed to his friend Robert Aiken) of exhibitionist false feeling. There is a difference between artifice and artificiality, between artistic discipline and the aping of fashionable modes of feeling, and Burns did not always recognise this.

There is a self-flattering aspect in the Kailyard's pictures of Scottish small-town life (though we may except Barrie from this) which distinguishes them from the benign pictures of farming life presented by Fergusson in 'The Farmer's Ingle' and by Burns in 'The Cotter's Saturday Night'. For all the occasional interpolations of an intrusive genteel sentimentality in Burns's poem, it, like Fergusson's, is rooted in an understanding of the reality of the working life of a farmer and his family. There may be a degree of idealisation in both poems, but it does not smother this reality. But if we consider, for example, the stories called 'A Lad o' Pairts' in *Beside the Bonnie Brier Bush* we see what became a stock picture of the humble but perceptive village dominie encouraging the bright local boy to higher things and, with the moral and financial support of the community, enabling him to go off to university. Young George Howe from Drumtochty, having been nurtured in the little local school by Domsie the dominie, goes off to win all the university prizes in Latin, Greek and other subjects. Here is a typical piece of dialogue. Domsie is recollecting his pupil's earlier history:

'It's ten years ago at the brak up o' the winter ye brought him down to me, Mrs Hoo, and ye said at the schule-house door, "Dinna be hard on him, Mister Jamieson, he's my only bairn, and a wee thingie quiet." Div ye mind what I said, "There's something ahint that face," and my heart warmed to George that hour. Two years after the Doctor examined the schule, and he looks at George, "That's a likely lad, Dominie. What think ye?" And he was only eight years auld, and no big for his size. "Doctor, I daurna prophesy till we turn him into the Latin, but a've my thoughts." So I had a' the time, but I never boasted; na, na, that's dangerous. Didna I say, "Ye hev a promisin' laddie, Whinnie," ae day in the market?'

'It's a fac',' said Whinnie, 'it was the day I bocht the white coo.' But Domsie swept on.

'The first year o' Latin was enough for me. He juist nippit up his verbs. Caesar couldna keep him going; he wes into Vergil afore he was eleven, and the Latin prose, man, as sure as a'm living, it tasted of Cicero frae the beginning.'

But the laid o' pairts sickens with some unspecified complaint and comes home from the university to die. On his death-bed he presents his Latin *Imitatio Christi* to the dominie and utters a final prayer for him: 'Lord Jesus, remember my dear maister, for he's been a kind freend to me and mony a puir laddie in Drumtochty. Bind up his sair heart and give him licht at eventide, and may the maister and his scholars meet some mornin' where the schule never skails, in the kingdom o' oor Father.'

Twice Domsie said Amen, and it seemed as the voice of another man, and then he kissed George upon the forehead; but what they said Marget did not wish to hear.

When he passed out at the garden gate, the westering sun was shining golden, and the face of Domsie was like unto that of a little child.

That gives the flavour of the Kailyard not unfairly. Barrie at least allowed his Sentimental Tommy to fail to win his bursary to Aberdeen University: the sentimentality of that book lay in other directions and there was no Scottish self-congratulation on the traditional Scottish lad o' pairts. Ian Maclaren is more typical of the sentimentally edifying pictures of Scottish life that filled magazines (such as *The British Weekly,* edited in London by a former Free Church minister from Aberdeen-shire) that printed fiction descriptive of Scottish life.

The reaction when it came was fierce. George Douglas Brown's novel, *The House with the Green Shutters,* published in 1901, did for the Kailyard what Crabbe's *The Village* did for Goldsmith's *Deserted Village,* describing Scottish pro-vincial life, as Crabbe described life in a Suffolk village, 'As Truth will paint it, and as Bards will not'. Brown's picture of the village of Barbie, based on his native Ochiltree, Ayrshire, is in many ways as one-sided as Ian Maclaren's picture of Drumtochty (which is Glen Almond): its collection of mean-spirited and malignant inhabitants is presented with almost masochistic fierceness, while those who are not mean-spirited, such as the principal character, the ruthless, ambitious and domineering John Gourlay, his sensitive and incompetent son and his broken-spirited wife, are in no position to challenge or change this quality in others. Gourlay's brutal self-seeking in the end destroys both himself and his family (his wife, son and daughter commit suicide jointly at the end of the book, after Gourlay himself has been ruined). There is a melodramatic quality in the novel and a sense of personal anger in it, which militates against its quality as a great novel. But nobody can deny its power. My point however is not to discuss the plot or the quality of *The House with the Green Shutters* but to cite it as one element in the reaction against the complex of attitudes associated with the sentimental strand in the genteel tradition. There is no self-flattering picture here of the lad o' pairts being encouraged by the local dominie and the local minister to go on to university where he beats the students who come from great city schools. Young John Gourlay *does* go to university, against the contemptuous advice of the uninterested dominie, because his father wants him to go for his own reasons. I quote only two passages. Here is the first:

> 'Get yourself ready for College in October,' he ordered his son that evening.
>
> 'The College!' cried John aghast.
>
> 'Yes! Is there anything in that to gape at?' snapped his father, in sudden irritation at the boy's amaze.
>
> 'But I don't want to gang!' John whimpered as before.
>
> 'Want! what does it matter what *you* want? You should be damned glad of the chance! I mean to make ye a minister; they have plenty of money and little to do—a grand, easy life o't. MacCandlish tells me you're a stupid ass, but have some little gift of words. You have every qualification!'
>
> 'It's against *my* will,' John bawled angrily.
>
> '*Your* will!' sneered his father.

The next quotation, from the end of the same chapter, gives the dominie's view:

> Old Bleach⁄the⁄boys, the bitter dominie (who rarely left the studies in political economy which he found a solace for his thwarted powers), happened to be at the Cross that evening. A brooding and taciturn man, he said nothing till others had their say. Then he shook his head.
>
> 'They're making a great mistake,' he said gravely, 'they're making a great mistake! Yon boy's the last boy on earth who should go to College.'
>
> 'Ay, man, dominie, he's an infernal ass, is he not?' they cried, and pressed for his judgment.
>
> At last, partly in real pedantry, partly with humorous intent to puzzle them, he delivered his astounding mind.
>
> 'The fault of young Gourlay,' quoth he, 'is a sensory perceptiveness in gross excess of his intellectuality.'
>
> They blinked and tried to understand.
>
> 'Ay man, dominie!' said Sandy Toddle. 'That means he's an infernal cuddy, dominie! Does it na, dominie?'
>
> But Bleach⁄the⁄boys had said enough. 'Ay,' he said dryly, 'there's a wheen gey cuddies in Barbie!' and he went back to his stuffy little room to study *The Wealth of Nations*.

The economic ruin of the older Gourlay is brought about by social and economic forces he does not understand, and in this respect he bears a certain resemblance to Michael Hen⁄shard in Hardy's *The Mayor of Casterbridge*. But George Douglas Brown lacked Hardy's epic vision. He anchors his story in a deliberately limited time and place and employs it consciously to confront the Kailyard. Its power is enormous and its effect was felt in waves that rolled across Scottish literature for generations: A. J. Cronin's *Hatter's Castle* is in some degree a re⁄writing of the novel three decades later in more modern terms.

Beside *The House with the Green Shutters* we must set J. MacDougall Hay's *Gillespie*, published in 1914, as another classic attack on the kailyard version of Scottish small-town and village life. It is set in Brieston, which is the west coast fishing village of Tarbert, and it is written with an almost diabolic force. Gillespie Strang, the principal character, ruth-less, ambitious, mercenary, miserly, is a man of evil in the sense that John Gourlay was not. Hay's novel is driven by a demonic religious force to expose the self-destructiveness of evil and the impotence of ordinary humane feelings to cope with it. Hay himself was a minister, and Francis Hart is surely right when he says that in this novel 'his attack on materialism and its weak sister humanitarianism is mounted from a neo-Calvinist prophetic perspective'.[2] Hay can be verbose and melodramatic and sometimes an obsessive tone rises from his pages. He is not protesting against mean-spiritedness and lack of compassion from any kind of secular modern morality. His attitude is not 'enlightened' in the sense that the eighteenth-century Moderates were enlightened. He is worlds away from any form of the genteel tradition. At the end of the novel Gillespie, with his wife and son dead under appalling conditions and his father dying, feels some sense of his own doom and some sense of remorse, but his father cannot hear him when he speaks words intended to make amends, and remains silent. 'It was beyond the power of mortal to break that profound quiet. Its judgment, the judgment of unearthly silence, had again found Gillespie, ringing with a mighty anvil-stroke of doom upon his soul the words, "Too late! too late!" He tottered from the bed, casting one last look of anguish upon the wearied face sunk in the pillows. In that moment he would have given gold and house and gear, if only one glimmer of tender recognition would divinely light those eyes and sweep across that face . . .'. He dies soon after, in agony, of lockjaw, unredeemed. There is no sociological or psychological explanation given of Gillespie's driving greed and unscrupulous cunning in pursuing his material fortune: there is talk of an ancient family curse working itself out, but this is not presented as anything real; what is real are the everyday life of this fishing village, pictured with a harsh vitality, the characters who impinge on Gillespie's life and activities, speaking a vigorous local Scots, and the central, doomed—even predestined, we sometimes feel—character of Gillespie himself. One feels that if the novel had been developed as a literary form in Scotland in the late seventeenth century, some passionate Calvinist might have written something like this. It is not so much anti-genteel as pre-genteel. It is quite unlike later novels of social realism which endeavour to expose unpleasant *and changeable* realities. Gillespie is what he is and drees his weird: he can no other.

Neither of the novels just discussed represents any part of the tradition of revolt against respectability and ideals of bourgeois success that we have seen in Robert Louis Stevenson. Of course both these novels exposed in different ways the precariousness and hollowness of the pursuit of material success which the Kailyard, with its belief in the lad o' pairts going out from his native village to conquer the world, had fostered. In this sense it is interesting that *Gillespie*, for all its neo-Calvinism, is very far indeed from the view, associated with some varieties of Calvinism, that worldly prosperity is both the deserved reward of hard work and a sign of God's grace. At the same time its attack on materialism is not made from the point of view of the Bohemian or even from the anti-Philistine position of Matthew Arnold. Attacks on middle-class values were a staple of Victorian fiction, while the Victorian prophets—Carlyle, Ruskin, Arnold, William Morris—each in his own way attacked bourgeois philistinism or materialism. The opposition of *la vie de Bohème* to the respectabilities of bourgeois society, which began in France and flourished in an artistic tradition throughout Europe; the desire to *épater les bourgeois,* to indulge in aesthetic exhibitionism, or to 'burn with a hard gem-like flame' while pursuing aesthetic experiences, are part of a rather different story. When anti-respectability raises its voice in authentic passion in twentieth-century Scotland, it echoes neither Stevenson nor the anti-kailyarders. It is associated with a contempt for the Establishment as representing a genteel anglicising of Scottish life and culture and a suspicion of all established reputations. Listen to this voice:

> My aim all along has been the most drastic *desuetisation* of Scottish life and letters . . . and getting rid of the whole gang of high mucky-mucks, famous fatheads, old wives of both sexes, stuffed shirts, hollow men with headpieces stuffed with straw, bird-wits, lookers-under-beds, trained seals, creeping Jesuses, Scots Wha-evers, village idiots, police-men, leaders of white-mouse factions, and what 'Billy' Phelps calls Medlar Novelists (the medlar being a fruit that becomes rotten before it is ripe), Commercial Calvin-ists, makers of 'noises like a turnip', and all the touts, toadies and lickspittles of the English Ascendancy, and their infernal women-folk, and all their skunkoil skul-duggery.

The same writer concludes his autobiography like this:

> And my last word here is that, if I had to choose a motto to be engraved under my name and the dates of my birth and death on my tombstone, it would be:
> 'A disgrace to the community.'—Mr Justice Mugge.

This is Christopher Murray Grieve, writing under his pen-name Hugh MacDiarmid, expressing, as he did so often and so vehemently, his total contempt for every kind of respect-ability and orthodoxy in the Scotland of his day. MacDiarmid was born in 1892 and died in 1978. He created a poetic renaissance in Scotland virtually single-handed, setting him-self against the debased Burns tradition of couthily senti-mental vernacular poetry in Scots, which had teetered on right through the nineteenth century and into the twentieth, crying 'Back to Dunbar' and ransacking the pages of Jamie-son's Scottish Dictionary for vivid Scots words that could be employed to render with cunning craftsmanship the subtlest and most difficult areas of Scottish experience. As a polemicist and a theorist MacDiarmid was wildly self-contradictory, thrashing around in anger and frustration in his attempt to find a viable tradition in Scottish culture which he could restore or re-create or invent. He was by temperament a system-builder, a lover of order with an almost mystical sense of the relation between the most trivial individual experience and the strange truths underlying the structure of the universe. He embraced both Communism and Scottish Nationalism, but neither in any orthodox sense. He praised David Hume as the greatest of Scotsmen, admiring the honesty and original-ity of his sceptical mind, yet he himself was at the core a religious man and also—further contradiction—he frequently expressed a violent contempt for the eighteenth-century Scot-tish *literati* (of whom Hume was one of the leaders) for their repudiation of their own Scots language, their truckling to a genteel anglicisation and their betrayal of their own national culture. He pleaded eloquently for the common man and expressed the wish that his poetry would be accessible to the workers, yet he wanted poetry to be difficult and inaccessible to the masses. He was aware of these contradictions. In his 'Second Hymn to Lenin' he wrote:

Are my poems spoken in the factories and fields,
  In the streets o' the toon?
Gin they're no, then I'm failin' to dae
  What I ocht to ha' dune.

Gin I canna win through to the man in the street,
  The wife by the hearth,
A' the cleverness on earth'll no' mak' up
  For the damnable dearth.

'Haud on, haud on; what poet's dune that?
  Is Shakespeare read,
Or Dante or Milton or Goethe or Burns?'
  —You heard what I said.

But he also wrote:

> It's no the purpose o' poetry to sing
> The beauty o' the dirt frae which we spring
> But to cairry us as fair as ever it can
> 'Yont nature and the Common Man.

And he wrote:

> I am horrified by the triviality of life, by its corruption
> and helplessness,
> No prospect of eternal life, no fullness of existence,
> no love without betrayal,
> No passion without satiety. Yet life could be beautiful
> even now.
> But all is soiled under philistine rule. What
> untouched spiritual powers
> Are hidden in the dark and cold, under
> the suffocating atmosphere
> Of philistine life, waiting for a better time when
> the first ray of light
> And breath of fresh air will call them to life and
> let them unfold?
> Civilisation has hitherto consisted in the
> diffusion and dilution
> Of habits arising in privileged centres. It has not sprung
> from the people.
> It has arisen in their midst by a variation from them
> And it has afterwards imposed itself on them from above.
> A state composed exclusively of such workers and peasants
> As make up most modern nations would
> be utterly barbarous.
> Every liberal tradition would perish in it. The
> national and historic
> Essence of patriotism itself would be lost, though
> the emotion no doubt
> Would endure, for it is not generosity that people lack.

They possess every impulse; it is experience
                              they cannot gather
For in gathering it they would be constituting
                              the higher organs
That make up an aristocratic society. Day,
                    the surrounding world, the life of men
Is entangled and meaningless; society is
                              the endless human triviality;
The judgment of the world pulls at the roots of
                              the best plants of life.
Man himself, aside from historic aggregations, is only
The shadow of a passing cloud, his very existence hardly
                              more than an illusion.
His thought resembles the ray of a fountain;
                              it rises, sparkles,
Reaches a certain height and falls, and begins
                              the process again.
—Would it were even beginning again in Scotland today!
There is no tyranny so hateful as a vulgar anonymous
                              tyranny like ours.
It is all permeating, all thwarting; it blasts every
                              budding novelty
And sprig of genius with its omnipresent
                              and fierce stupidity.

These words, from the volume *Stony Limits and Other Poems*, produced in what might be called MacDiarmid's middle period, the first phase of his English-writing as distinct from his earlier Scots-writing period, show clearly enough the dilemma of a poet seeking desperately for a tradition within which to work. As a Scottish poet passionately committed to Scotland, MacDiarmid fought hard against the lack of continuity in the Scottish poetic tradition, a lack that goes right back to the departure of the Court in 1603. He also saw himself as a world poet, in touch with and forming a union with all the great poets of his time from America to China and with the great poets of the past too. But his universalism was based on Scotland and spoke from Scotland. His problem was, with what kind of voice should the Scottish poet speak? In his first great creative phase, which many consider his greatest, he turned to a Scots language made up quite deliberately of words borrowed from the old makars or looked up in Jamieson's Dictionary. He was trying to distil a poetic tradition in a vacuum, and he was marvellously successful in this impossible-seeming task. Repudiating the simplicities of Scots dialect poetry—most of it nostalgic, much of it written by exiled Scots, such as Charles Murray, remembering their rural Scottish background from abroad, and some of it skilfully and even movingly done—MacDiarmid tried to write as though there had been no break in the Scottish literary tradition and no disintegration of the Scots literary language. And, incredibly, he succeeded. Here is a little poem from *Sangschaw* (1925):

Ae weet forenicht i' the yow-trummle
I saw yon antrin thing,
A watergaw wi' its chitterin' licht
Ayont the on-ding;
An' I thocht o' the last wild look ye gied
Afore ye deed!

There was nae reek i' the laverock's hoose
That nicht—an' nane i' mine;
But I hae thocht o' that foolish licht
Ever sin' syne;
An' I think that mebbe at last I ken
What your look meant then.

When this poem by Hugh MacDiarmid first appeared in *Scottish Chapbook,* edited by C. M. Grieve, the editor commented on his own poem as follows:

Doric economy of expressiveness is impressively illustrated in the first four lines of Mr MacDiarmid's poem. Translate them into English. That is the test. You will find that the shortest possible translation runs something like this 'One wet afternoon (or early evening) in the cold weather in July after the sheep-shearing I saw that rare thing—an indistinct rainbow, with its shivering light, above the heavily-falling rain.'

'Yow-trummle' is 'ewe-tremble', because in the sudden spell of cold weather the newly-sheared sheep tremble with cold. It is a marvellously expressive word, re-discovered by Mac-Diarmid. A laverock is a lark, and MacDiarmid himself explained 'There was nae reek i' the laverock's house' as meaning 'It was a dark and stormy night.'

MacDiarmid's masterpiece is his Scots poem-sequence *A Drunk Man looks at the Thistle* (1926). I have described this remarkable work at length elsewhere, and given my critical appraisal of it. Here my point is to cite it as an example of what can be done by a poet of genius determined to create his own poetic tradition as he moves. For MacDiarmid is not signifi-cant only as the great anti-genteel poet, the poet in revolt against everything esteemed and respected by the society of his time. He is much more significant for what he achieved in poetry by his thrashing around trying to find a mode in which to operate. Any variety of the genteel tradition, including the debased post-Burns Scots tradition, was seen by him as no tradition at all, only a pretence of one.

Literary historians have little difficulty in tracing the muta-tions of the English poetic tradition from Chaucer to, shall we say, T. S. Eliot. We see the decline of the Chaucerian mode, the emergence of new fashions and forms in Tudor poetry, the efflorescence of Elizabethan poetry, and we know the influences at work and the aims followed. We can see the relationship between Elizabethan imagery and metaphysical conceit; we can trace the Jonsonian tradition, see how it mutated into the Cavalier tradition, and follow it after that. We know about 'the refinement of our numbers', we can see what Dryden was doing and what Pope was doing after him, and we can follow the stream into the varieties of eighteenth-century poetry until we come to what we call the Romantic Movement. Critics and scholars will of course disagree about the precise nature of individual movements and even on whether a particular movement ever really existed as a movement; but they agree that there is flow and there are causes, there is action and reaction. We can see the relation between Keats and Tennyson and between Tennyson and the pre-Raphaelites. We know how Hopkins differed from the other Victorians and why; we can trace precisely the movement of W. B. Yeats from dreamy late Romantic to a fiercely individual symbolic-metaphysical poet. We know what Eliot revolted against and why; who and what influenced him; and what his influence has been. I cite these commonplaces only to point the contrast with Scottish poetry. Here there is no such traceable tradition. We can see what happened, but what happened is not the mutations of a tradition: it is a series of compensations for a lack of one, or a series of adjustments between an English tradition and the orts and fragments of a Scottish tradition, or a precariously balanced personal tightrope-walking act.

So MacDiarmid, driven by his passion for penetrating to the roots of the Scottish experience and relating his discovery to a vision of the world and indeed of the universe, moved from phase to phase, from style to style, from language to language. After those haunting Scots lyrics of which 'The Watergaw' is an example, and after the astonishing experiment of a Scots comic-epic in *A Drunk Man,* we find poetry like this (the opening of 'On a Raised Beach'):

All is lithogenesis—or lochia,
Carpolite fruit of the forbidden tree,
Stones blacker than any in the Caaba,
Cream-coloured caen-stone, chatoyant pieces,
Celadon and corbeau, bistre and beige,

Glaucous, hoar, enfouldered, cyathiform,
Making mere faculae of the sun and moon . . .

This strange and memorable poem presents the reality of
natural objects as something permanently outside man, as
existing objectively in their self-sufficient neutrality, and as
such challenging human observation and imagination. It is
the exact opposite of the Wordsworthian position. Later in
the poem he falls into a more natural English:

We must be humble. We are so easily baffled by appearances
And do not realise that these stones are one with the stars.
It makes no difference to them whether they are high or low,
Mountain peak or ocean floor, palace or pigsty.
There are plenty of ruined buildings in the world but
no ruined stones.

Later MacDiarmid moved on to a kind of stitched-together
catalogue poetry, citing whole paragraphs from works of
scholars and scientists and even from articles in newspapers,
pillaging right and left with a parade of diverse knowledge
that was really more of a reflection of his magpie mind than
evidence of universal scholarship. He quotes dozens of
languages—even, in *In Memoriam James Joyce,* quoting a couple
of words in Hebrew, using Hebrew letters but printing them
upside down (a fact of which he was totally unaware until I
pointed it out to him), stringing out long Whitmanesque
catalogues of names and facts, trying to bring the world of fact
and the interpretations of that world made by scientists into
poetry. There is a note almost of desperation in this aim. He
himself was perfectly aware of what he was doing, and of how
strange it would seem to many, how upsetting to those who
saw his perfectly wrought early lyrics in Scots as the peak of
his achievement. *In Memoriam James Joyce* is subtitled 'From a
Vision of World Language' (title of a longer poem which he
never completed) and this gives evidence of his desire to go
beyond any discoverable Scottish tradition to something

absolute, an attempt, as it were, to short-circuit the whole business of a poetic tradition. He described the poem in a passage within the poem:

> Hence this *hapax legomenon* of a poem, this exercise
> In schablone, bordatini, and prolonged scordatura,
> This *divertissement philologique,*
> This Wortspiel, this torch symphony,
> This 'liberal education', this collection of *fonds de tiroir,*
> This—even more than Kierkegaard's
> 'Frygt og Baeven'—'dialectical lyric',
> This rag-bag, this Loch Ness monster, this impact
> Of the whole range of *Weltliteratur* on one man's brain,
> In short, this 'friar's job', as they say in Spain
> Going back in kind
> To the Eddic 'Converse of Thor and the All-Wise Dwarf'
> (Al-viss Mal, 'Edda die lieden des Codex Regius', 120, 1f)
> [and here MacDiarmid has a footnote: 'Text,
>   G. Neckel, Heidelberg, 1914']
> Existing in its present MS form
> Over five centuries before Shakespeare.
> You remember it?

Other Scottish poets followed MacDiarmid in his use of revived literary Scots drawn from older works and from dictionaries as well as from surviving spoken Scots. But MacDiarmid founded no tradition. How could he, when he spent his life trying unsuccessfully to find one? His poetic career shows how it is possible to write great poetry if you lack a poetic tradition provided you know what you are doing and exactly where you are. His friend and fellow poet Norman MacCaig once said to him (in my hearing), when Mac-Diarmid was boasting of having established a poetic renais-sance: 'Chris, you are a great poet, but a great poet is not a *literature.*'

Other distinguished Scottish poets of our century have written in English. Edwin Muir wrote solely in English. So does Norman MacCaig. But in each case it is English with a Scots accent, even though the poetic modes they used are derived from the English and Anglo-American tradition. MacCaig believes he can do without a tradition and depend on his own insights, his feeling for words and his knowledge of other poetry. And indeed he has produced some fine poetry combining quiet observation of the external world with subtle and sometimes witty speculation. Perhaps with so many cultural traditions in a state of flux throughout the western world every man must make his own terms with his medium. But this raises questions beyond the scope of these lectures.

Sydney Goodsir Smith was born in New Zealand but learned Edinburgh Scots on the streets of Edinburgh after his family had settled there. He then learned from MacDiarmid to extend his Scots vocabulary from older literary and from lexicographic sources. He was very much more an urban poet than MacDiarmid, in spite of some delicate lyrics set in the Scottish countryside and on the seashore, and his nose-thumbing at the conventions was more in the tradition of urban bohemianism than of MacDiarmid's metaphysical scorn for the inevitable mediocrity of what was established and successful. There was something of the old Goliardic tradition in Sydney Smith: this tradition in fact lingered on in Scottish universities after many other older traditions had disappeared. A poet of skill and sometimes of passion, Smith found himself able cheerfully to accept a kind of willed Scots, becoming a poet of Scottish national consciousness (as in his play *Wallace*) by volition. He could not have written as he did if MacDiarmid had not written in Scots, but he lacked MacDiarmid's questing mind.

Sydney Smith built up his own Bohemian world centred on the pubs of Edinburgh's Rose Street, notably the Abbotsford. In the years immediately after the Second World War these pubs often saw drunken poets celebrating their non-respectable habits with deliberate bravado. Whether this indicated a malaise in Scottish culture or represented the natural exuberance of young poets relishing their individuality is a point that has been argued at some length by a variety of observers. But heavy drinking in pubs does not really constitute a viable poetic tradition. MacDiarmid was a drinker too, and held court at the Abbotsford and at Milne's Bar for many years, but his desperate search for an order within which to write his poetry went on despite that.

Some modern Scottish poets have settled for a local urban poetry written in a Scots which, while partly drawn from older literature, is firmly rooted in the surviving spoken Scots of the city. The most distinguished of these is Robert Garioch (R. G. Sutherland), who was influenced by another Edin-burgh poet, the eighteenth-century Robert Fergusson. He has a fine poem entitled simply 'To Robert Fergusson' in which he expresses his sense of the disparity between Fergusson's city and his own together with his awareness that the present is moving traditionless into an unfurnished world. The poem opens:

> Fergusson, tho twa-hunder year
> Awa, your image is mair clear
> nor monie things that nou appear
> in braid daylicht.
> What gars perspective turn sae queer?
> What ails my sicht?
>
> Pairtlie, nae dout, because your een
> gey clearlie saw the Embro scene
> in times whan Embro was a queen
> sae weill worth seein
> that life wi' her still had a wheen
> guid things worth preein . . .

The forty-six stanza poem (the stanza is the old Habbie Sim-son stanza, which Fergusson used as well as Burns) ends with a reluctant move back into the present:

Robert, fareweill; I maun awa.
My gait is stey, no wyce ava,
by Jacob's Ladder, Burns's smaa
          Greek pepperpat,
Sanct Andrew's Hous an' aa an' aa—
          nae mair o' that!

Pechan, I turn, whilst aye your leid
Of lowan Scots sounds in my heid
wi levan braith, tho ye ligg died;
          I glowre faur doun
and see the waesom wrak outspreid
          of your auld toun.

Syne trauchlan up the brae yince mair,
frae Canogait, I leave ye there,
what wee white roses scent the air
          about your grave,
and til some suburb new and bare
          gang wi' the lave.

Some of Garioch's most interesting work is his translation of
Roman dialect sonnets—*I Sonetti Romaneschi*—of the nineteenth-century Italian poet Giuseppe Belli. Here he adapts a
fine and flexible Scots, drawn from a variety of sources, to
Belli's racy Romanesque vocabulary, and the matching is
perfect. This is the kind of situation where problems of literary
tradition fade away: the Scots dialect poet and the Roman
dialect poet meet in a common desire to preserve the life of a
dialect that has been ousted by the dominant language. But
the Belli-Garioch coalition fits my theme perfectly: both the
Roman originals and the Scots versions are deliberately, pro-
vocatively, anti-genteel. One of the functions left for dialect
was nose-thumbing. And both Belli and Garioch use one of
the oldest of courtly verse-forms, the sonnet, to thumb their
noses at both the courtly and the genteel tradition.

We think of the courtly sonnets of the Renaissance, we think of the attitude to the King in Scottish courtly poetry, and we see in this Belli-Garioch sonnet how after nearly four hundred years the tradition has been turned on its head: here is Garioch's rendering of Belli's sonnet, *Li soprani der monno vechio*:

The Rulers of the Auld Warld

Yince on a time there was a King, wha sat
screivan this edict in his palace-haa
til aa his fowk: 'Vassals, I tell ye flat
that I am I, and you are buggar-aa.

I mak richt wrang, wrang richt, my word is law:
I can sell yese, sae muckle fir the lot:
If I hing yese, ye're no ill-yaised ava,
ye rent yir lives and gear frae me, that's that.

Whasae bides in this warld, bot the title
either of Paip, or Emperor, or King,
sall nivir mell in oniething that's vital.'

The heidsman tuke this edict roun in sicht
of aa the fowk, speiran anent this thing,
and they aa said til him: *That's richt, that's richt.*

In my discussion of the Scots literary tradition I have talked mostly of poetry, and only brought in fiction to illustrate the Kailyard movement and the reaction to it. An adequate study of Scottish fiction would have to take in all sorts of considera-tion beyond the scope of these lectures. At least we now have a serious and scholarly study of the subject in Francis Hart's book *The Scottish Novel*. The problems of tradition are on the whole different and more complex with fiction, and the attempt to discover a viable modern Scottish fictional tradi-tion, notably in Lewis Grassic Gibbon's trilogy *A Scots Quair*, is worth extended examination. But that would take us far away indeed from the consequences of the departure of the Court in 1603. There was no tradition of Scottish fictional prose established by the time Scots ceased to be regarded as a 'high' literary language, and with some exceptions it was only in the dialogue of novels, where spoken speech was imitated, that Scots prose could survive. By the time the novel emerged there was no courtly tradition of any kind left in Scotland. But as the novel was essentially a bourgeois literary form anyway this was of no significance. However, the novel in Scotland is involved at some points with gentility, especially in its sentimental varieties, and with the revolt against this. The greatest cry against gentility of all kinds in Scotland was that raised by MacDiarmid, and I cannot do better than close with a few of his lines which strike at the cherished belief in the desirability of happiness that all decent people have professed for generations:

To hell wi' happiness!
I sing the terrifying discipline
O' the free mind that gars a man
Mak' his joys kill his joys, . . .

When the organically developed discipline of an art form is not available, the task of recovering discipline in emotion and its expression is indeed 'terrifying'.

NOTES
1. Eric Anderson, 'The Kailyard School', in Ian Campbell, Ed., *Nineteenth Century Scottish Fiction,* Manchester, 1979, p.134.
2. Francis Hart, *The Scottish Novel,* Cambridge, Mass., 1978, pp.137-8.

INDEX

accents, genteel, 71
Addison, Joseph, 1, 68
admiration, 4, 5, 11
admonition, 4, 5, 11, 12
American speech, 69
Anderson, Eric, 84
anglicisation, 20, 24
'antisyzygy', 76
Ariosto, *Orlando Furioso*, 17
Arnold, Matthew, 91
Auchinleck, Lord, 73
Austen, Jane, 1
Ayton, Sir Robert: as a
  Cavalier poet, 24–9, 41, 42;
  poem on River Tweed, 25;
  Scots sonnet, 24–5
    works cited
'Did you ever see the day', 25–6
'Old–Long–syne', 26, 28

ballad(s): absence of, in
  Watson's collection, 43–4;
  love, 21; singing, 7, 8
balladry, popular, 9
Bannatyne, George, 4, 10, 17,
  35, 38
Barrie, J. M.: and Kailyard
  fiction, 85, 87
    works cited
Auld Licht Idylls, 84
A Window in Thrums, 84
The Little Minister, 84

bawdry: decline in, 76; in 16th
  c., 7; in 18th c., 72; Pro–
  testant attitude to, 8; *The
  Merry Muses of Caledonia*, 72
Baxter, Charles, 78, 79–83, 84
Beattie, James, *Scotticisms*, 68–9
Belli, Giuseppe, 103–4
Bible, language of the, 30
'Blythesome Wedding, The', 36
Boyd, Mark Alexander, 23–4
Braxfield, Lord, 73, 77
broadsides, 37, 40, 42, 44
Brodie, Deacon, 76–7
Brown, George Douglas, *The
  House with the Green Shutters*,
  87–9
Buchanan, George, 13
Burel, John, 40–1
Burlesque style, 55–7
Burns, Robert: and the Croch–
  allan Fencibles, 72, 74; Ayr–
  shire Scots of, 62–3, 65;
  balance of Scots and English
  in, 55, 65–6; collection of
  bawdy songs, 72; English and
  Scots pronunciation in, 38;
  epistolary style of, 61–2; genteel
  tradition in, 59–62, 63–5, 74;
  language of, 57, 59–65;
  pastoralism, 22; speech of, 62;
  use of stanza form, 35, 37;
  view of Fergusson, 59

107